READING/WRITING COMPANION

Mc
Graw
Hill
Education

COVER: Nathan Love, Erwin Madrid

mheducation.com/prek-12

Copyright © McGraw-Hill Education

All rights reserved. No part of this publication may be
reproduced or distributed in any form or by any means,
or stored in a database or retrieval system, without the
prior written consent of McGraw-Hill Education,
including, but not limited to, network storage or
transmission, or broadcast for distance learning.

Send all inquiries to:
McGraw-Hill Education
Two Penn Plaza
New York, NY 10121

ISBN: 978-0-07-901856-4
MHID: 0-07-901856-4

Printed in the United States of America.

3 4 5 6 7 8 9 LMN 23 22 21 20 19   B

Welcome to Wonders!

Read exciting **Literature**, **Science**, and **Social Studies** texts!

★ **LEARN** about the world around you!

★ **THINK**, **SPEAK**, and **WRITE** about genres!

★ **COLLABORATE** in discussion and inquiry!

★ **EXPRESS** yourself!

my.mheducation.com
Use your student login to read core texts, practice grammar and spelling, explore research projects and more!

GENRE STUDY 1 NARRATIVE NONFICTION

GENRE STUDY 2 REALISTIC FICTION

GENRE STUDY **3** **ARGUMENTATIVE TEXT**

WRAP UP THE UNIT

 Digital Tools Find this eBook and other resources at **my.mheducation.com**

JGI Jamie Grill/Blend Images/Getty Images

GENRE STUDY 1 **EXPOSITORY TEXT**

GENRE STUDY 2 **FOLKTALE**

Yulia Reznikov/Alamy

GENRE STUDY 3 POETRY

WRAP UP THE UNIT

 Digital Tools Find this eBook and other resources at **my.mheducation.com**

Peter Zander/Workbook Stock/Getty Images

Talk About It

Essential Question

How can experiencing nature change the way you think about it?

You don't have to be a naturalist to have an amazing encounter with nature. There are natural wonders underground, such as caves, that display amazing formations. Above ground, you can find surprises while hiking among trees. California redwoods, for example, can grow to be over 320 feet tall!

Look at the photograph. Talk to a partner about what you see and what the hiker might be experiencing. Then describe a personal experience you had in nature and how it affected you. Fill in the chart with ways in which nature can affect people.

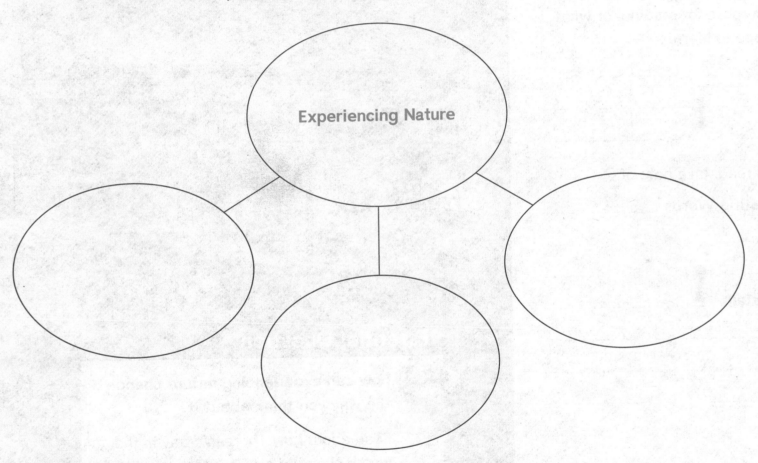

Experiencing Nature

Go online to **my.mheducation.com** and read the "Protecting Our Parks" Blast. Think about your experiences with nature. Why are parks important to society? Then blast back your response.

TAKE NOTES

Deciding on a purpose, or reason, for reading will help you focus on the text's topic. Preview the text by reading the title and headings and studying the pictures. Then write your purpose for reading, or what you hope to learn.

_____

_____

_____

As you read, take note of:

Interesting Words _____

_____

_____

Key Details _____

_____

_____

_____

_____

_____

_____

A Life in the Woods

Essential Question

How can experiencing nature change the way you think about it?

Read about how Thoreau's stay in the woods changed his view of nature.

(bkgd) DenisTangneyJr/iStock/Getty Images; Aaron Foster/Photographer's

FPG /Taxi/Getty Images

Into the Woods

Henry David Thoreau raised his pen to write, but the chatter of guests in the next room filled his ears. He stared at the page. "Concord, 1841" was all that he had written. How would he write a book with such noise in his family's house? Thoreau headed outside, shutting the door with **emphasis**. He would have to find a place of his own.

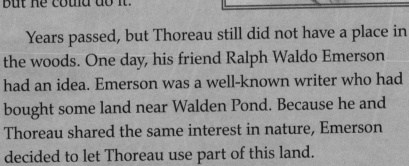

Thoreau walked out of town. Tall white pines soon replaced the painted houses. He listened to the rustling of the leaves. What if I could stay here, he thought. He could live off the land, close to nature, and begin his book. It would take work, but he could do it.

Years passed, but Thoreau still did not have a place in the woods. One day, his friend Ralph Waldo Emerson had an idea. Emerson was a well-known writer who had bought some land near Walden Pond. Because he and Thoreau shared the same interest in nature, Emerson decided to let Thoreau use part of this land.

In March of 1845, Thoreau began to build a cabin. By July, it was ready. He could live and write in the woods.

FIND TEXT EVIDENCE

Read

Paragraphs 1–2
Cause and Effect
What was the effect of Thoreau walking out of town? **Underline** the text evidence.

_____

_____

Homographs
The word _leaves_ has more than one meaning. **Draw a box** around context clues that give the meaning.

Paragraphs 3–4
Ask and Answer Questions
What question can you ask and answer about Thoreau?

_____

_____

Reread

Author's Craft

How does the author help you visualize Thoreau's experience as he walks out of town?

FIND TEXT EVIDENCE

Read

Paragraph 1

Ask and Answer Questions

What is a question you can ask and answer about Thoreau?

_____

_____

_____

Paragraphs 2–3

Cause and Effect

Circle the signal word that helps you identify why Thoreau thinks the loon is laughing at him. Then **underline** what caused him to think this.

Primary Sources

Look at the text from Thoreau's journal. What impressed him?

_____

_____

Reread

Author's Craft

Why might the author have included Thoreau's journal here?

Cabin Life

Thoreau's move to the woods **indicated** that he liked to be alone. But Thoreau did not feel that way. "I have a great deal of company in my house," he wrote. Red squirrels woke him by running up and down the **sheer** sides of his cabin. A snowshoe hare lived in the **debris** under his cabin, thumping against the floorboards. A sparrow once perched on his shoulder. Thoreau recorded these experiences in his journal. How easily writing came to him with the beauty of nature around him!

On Walden Pond

Thoreau was a **naturalist**. He noticed the habits of animals. Each **encounter** showed him something new. One afternoon, Thoreau tried to get a close look at a loon, but the bird quickly dove into the pond. He knew loons could travel long distances under water, so he guessed where it would come up. But every time Thoreau paddled to one spot, the loon came up somewhere else and let out a call—a howling laugh. What a silly loon, Thoreau thought. But after a while, Thoreau felt as though the bird was laughing at him because he still could not catch up to it. Thoreau wrote in his journal:

His white breast, the stillness of the air, and the smoothness of the water were all against him. At length he uttered one of those prolonged howls, as if calling on the god of the loons to aid him, and immediately there came a wind from the east and rippled the surface, and filled the whole air with misty rain, and I was impressed.

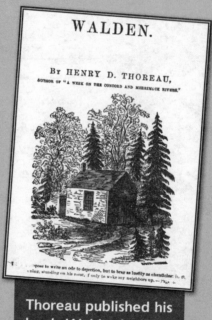

WALDEN.

BY HENRY D. THOREAU,

AUTHOR OF "A WEEK ON THE CONCORD AND MERRIMACK RIVERS."

Thoreau published his book *Walden* in 1854.

Loons are still a common sight on Walden Pond.

The **spectacular** scene made Thoreau wonder at the loon. It no longer seemed a silly animal, but one with some mysterious power. As months went by, Thoreau also became aware of each animal's ability to stay alive. "His power of observation seemed to indicate additional senses," Emerson once remarked. In winter, as he warmed his cabin by fire, he watched in awe as the moles warmed their nest by their own body heat. He understood forest life as never before.

Back to Concord

Like the geese that move to new ponds at the season's end, so too did Thoreau leave Walden. He had done what he had set out to do, and had learned much from the woods around him. He packed his few belongings and his stack of journals and returned to Concord. Now, he would turn his journal entries into a book. **Generations** to come would know life on Walden Pond!

Summarize

Use your notes to write a summary of Thoreau's experience living by Walden Pond.

NARRATIVE NONFICTION

FIND TEXT EVIDENCE

Read

Paragraph 1

Cause and Effect

Write a sentence that explains what caused Thoreau to understand "forest life as never before."

_____

_____

Paragraph 2

Ask and Answer Questions

What question can you ask to check your understanding of the second paragraph? Write your question.

_____

_____

Underline text evidence that helps you answer your question.

Reread

Author's Craft

How does the author show that Thoreau has changed by the end?

Vocabulary

Use the example sentences to talk with a partner about each word. Then answer the questions.

debris

The science class picked up **debris** that had washed up on the beach.

What is a synonym for debris?

_____

_____

emphasis

When Elena said, "Shhh," she put her finger to her lips for **emphasis**.

How can you show emphasis when you talk?

_____

_____

encounter

During a hike, you might have an **encounter** with a butterfly.

What is a synonym for encounter?

_____

_____

generations

My grandma has a pie recipe that has been in my family for many **generations**.

What is something students of your generation like to do?

_____

_____

indicated

The thermostat **indicated** that it was hot outside.

What is a synonym for indicated?

_____

_____

 Build Your Word List Pick a word you found interesting in the selection you read. Look up synonyms and antonyms of the word in a thesaurus and write them in your writer's notebook.

naturalist

The **naturalist** told us about many of the plants and animals she studied.

What is something you might ask a naturalist?

_____

_____

_____

sheer

When we looked up at the **sheer** rock wall, we knew it would be impossible to climb.

What else might you describe as sheer?

_____

_____

_____

spectacular

The mountaintop provides **spectacular** views.

What else might you describe as spectacular?

_____

_____

Homographs

Homographs are words that are spelled the same but have different meanings and may be pronounced differently. Use sentence clues to help you choose the correct meaning and pronunciation of a homograph. A dictionary can also help you with finding the meaning and pronunciation of the word.

🔍 FIND TEXT EVIDENCE

When I read the fourth sentence of "On Walden Pond" on page 4, I see a word that has two meanings: dove. I can use the phrase dove into the pond _to help me choose the correct meaning. That also helps me figure out the right way to say the word._

Thoreau tried to get a close look at the loon, but the bird quickly dove into the pond.

Your Turn Use sentence clues to figure out the meanings of the following homographs in "A Life in the Woods."

felt, page 4 _____

wind, page 4 _____

Ask and Answer Questions

When you read, you can ask yourself questions to monitor, or check, your understanding. Asking and then finding the answers to questions such as *What just happened?* or *Why did that happen?* will help you deepen your understanding of the text and gain knowledge. You can also ask and answer questions about the whole selection.

 FIND TEXT EVIDENCE

After you read the first paragraph of "A Life in the Woods" on page 3, you might ask yourself: *Why did Thoreau have to find a place of his own?* Reread the paragraph to find the answer.

Quick Tip

You can use headings to help you find the section where the answer to your question might be. Think about what kind of information will most likely answer your question. Then look for the section that has that information.

> **Page 3**
>
> **Into the Woods**
>
> Henry David Thoreau raised his pen to write, but the chatter of guests in the next room filled his ears. He stared at the page. "Concord, 1841" was all that he had written. How would he write a book with such noise in his family's house? Thoreau headed outside, shutting the door with **emphasis**. He would have to find a place of his own.

I read that Thoreau wondered how he could write a book with such noise in his family's house. From this I can infer that Thoreau needed to find a place of his own because the noise in his family's house made it impossible for him to write.

 Your Turn Reread "Back to Concord" on page 5. Ask a question that will help you check your understanding. How can you find the answer?

_____

_____

Primary and Secondary Sources

The selection "A Life in the Woods" is a narrative nonfiction text. Narrative nonfiction gives facts about real people and events. It tells a true story with a beginning, middle, and end. It may include both primary and secondary sources.

FIND TEXT EVIDENCE

I can tell that "A Life in the Woods" is narrative nonfiction. It gives facts about a real person, Henry David Thoreau, using primary and secondary sources. It also tells a story about how Thoreau was able to write a book about his experiences at Walden Pond.

Readers to Writers

One reason authors use primary sources such as journals and letters is so the reading audience can hear directly from people who experienced the events. This makes the writing more interesting and helps the reader to better understand the subject matter. Good authors make sure that their primary sources are credible, or believable. How can you use this feature in your own writing?

Page 4

Cabin Life

Thoreau's move to the woods **indicated** that he liked to be alone. But Thoreau did not feel that way. "I have a great deal of company in my house," he wrote. Red squirrels woke him by running up and down the **sheer** sides of his cabin. A snowshoe hare lived in the **debris** under his cabin, thumping against the floorboards. A sparrow once perched on his shoulder. Thoreau recorded these experiences in his journal. How easily writing came to him with the beauty of nature around him!

On Walden Pond

Thoreau was a **naturalist**. He noticed the habits of animals. Each **encounter** showed him something new. One afternoon, Thoreau tried to get a close look at a loon, but the bird quickly dove into the pond. He knew loons could travel long distances under water, so he guessed where it would come up. But every time Thoreau paddled to one spot, the loon came up somewhere else and let out a call—a howling laugh. What a silly loon, Thoreau thought. But after a while, Thoreau felt as though the bird was laughing at him because he still could not catch up to it. Thoreau wrote in his journal:

His white breast, the stillness of the air, and the smoothness of the water were all against him. At length he uttered one of those prolonged howls, as if calling on the god of the loons to aid him, and immediately there came a wind from the east and rippled the surface, and filled the whole air with misty rain, and I was impressed.

WALDEN.

By HENRY D. THOREAU,

Thoreau published his book *Walden* in 1854.

Secondary Source

A secondary source retells or interprets information from a primary source.

Primary Source

A primary source provides first-hand information about a topic. Autobiographies, journals, and letters are examples.

Your Turn Reread the passage "Cabin Life" on page 4. Find a sentence that comes from a primary source. How is a primary source unique?

_____

_____

_____

_____

Cause and Effect

To explain how and why things happen, authors may organize information to show cause and effect. A **cause** is an event or action that makes something happen. An **effect** is what happens as the result of a cause. Sometimes signal words and phrases such as *because, so,* and *as a result* are used to link ideas and show cause-and-effect relationships.

Quick Tip

If there are no signal words, you can use the following to help you identify cause-and-effect relationships in the text:

Because of this:

_____

Thoreau did this:

_____

🔍 FIND TEXT EVIDENCE

When I read the section "Into the Woods" from "A Life in the Woods" on page 3, I can look for signal words that show cause-and-effect relationships. I see the signal word because *in the sentence, "Because he and Thoreau shared the same interest in nature, Emerson decided to let Thoreau use part of this land."*

Cause	⟶	Effect
Emerson and Thoreau shared an interest in nature.	⟶	Emerson let Thoreau use his land.

Your Turn Reread "A Life in the Woods." Find cause-and-effect relationships and list them in your graphic organizer on page 11.

DenisTangneyJr/iStock/Getty Images

Cause	→	Effect
	→	
	→	
	→	

Respond to Reading

COLLABORATE

Discuss the prompt below. Think about how the author helped you understand Thoreau's experience at Walden Pond. Use your notes and graphic organizer. Make sure your central, or main, idea is clear and supported by details from the text.

How does the author help you understand the effect nature had on Thoreau?

_____

_____

_____

_____

_____

_____

_____

_____

_____

_____

_____

_____

Quick Tip

Use these sentence starters to discuss the text and to organize ideas.

- *The author uses a cause and effect structure to . . .*
- *Thoreau discovered that nature . . .*
- *In the end, Thoreau . . .*

Readers to Writers

When you write about a text, it is important to use information from that text to support your ideas. Using text evidence helps your readers know that your response is appropriate. It also helps you to know whether or not you understand the text. If you can't find evidence to support your ideas, then you may need to revise your response.

Relevant Information

When doing research, you look for information that is relevant, or appropriate, for your topic. The following will help you identify relevant information.

- Write a main idea question or statement for your project to help you focus on information connected to your topic.
- Enter key words that focus on your topic in a search engine.

If you need more help, ask a trusted adult to help you develop a research plan that includes identifying relevant information.

What is another idea you could use to look for relevant

information?_____

_____

Old Faithful geyser erupts about every 94 minutes.

COLLABORATE

Create a Promotional Map Work collaboratively with a group and develop a plan to create a map that promotes, or encourages, people to visit a national park. Your map can be drawn on paper or digitally created. Include features such as

- insets—small maps or pictures on or next to your larger map to show more detail of places in the park
- symbols for attractions, roads, trails, and other places
- a legend, or key, to identify symbols

With your group, develop a research plan using reliable sources of information such as the National Park Service website. After you finish your map, you will be sharing your work with the class.

 Tech Tip

If you want to create your map digitally, ask your teacher to show you a mapmaking program. The National Park Service website also includes different kinds of maps of park roads, trails, and attractions.

Lorcel/Shutterstock.com

Camping with the President

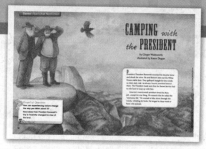

Literature Anthology:
pages 10–25

? **How does the author help you visualize what President Roosevelt sees and hears at Yosemite?**

Talk About It Reread **Literature Anthology** pages 16–17. Turn to a partner and discuss how the author describes what President Roosevelt experiences.

Cite Text Evidence What words and phrases help you create mental images about what President Roosevelt sees and hears? Write text evidence in the chart.

Text Evidence	What I Visualize

Write The author helps me visualize what Roosevelt sees and hears by

_____

_____

_____

_____

How does the author help you understand why President Roosevelt decides to help John Muir?

Talk About It Reread **Literature Anthology** page 19. Turn to your partner and discuss how President Roosevelt reacts to what John Muir tells him.

Cite Text Evidence How does the author help you see how Roosevelt feels about the sequoia trees being cut down? Write text evidence in the chart.

✂ **Evaluate Information**

Evaluate, or decide, which details are important to understanding how Roosevelt feels about the sequoia trees being cut down. Evaluating the details you read will help you determine key ideas.

Text Evidence	What He Plans To Do

Write I understand why Roosevelt helps Muir because the author

_____

_____

_____

_____

? How does the author's use of dialogue help you understand how President Roosevelt is affected by his night in the forest?

Talk About It Reread **Literature Anthology** pages 22–23. Turn to a partner and talk about what President Roosevelt said.

Cite Text Evidence What does President Roosevelt say that shows how he feels? Write text evidence in the web.

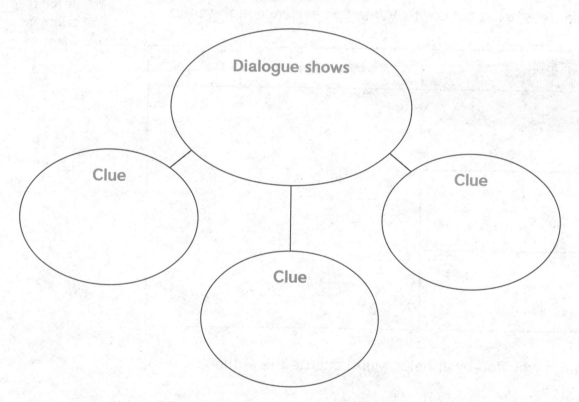

Dialogue shows

Clue

Clue

Clue

Write The author uses dialogue to help me understand that Roosevelt feels _____

_____

_____

Respond to Reading

COLLABORATE

Discuss the prompt below. Think about President Roosevelt's reaction to all the different areas that he visited in the Yosemite area. Use your notes and graphic organizer.

Think about what President Roosevelt said and did while at Yosemite. How does the author show how Roosevelt changes because of his experience?

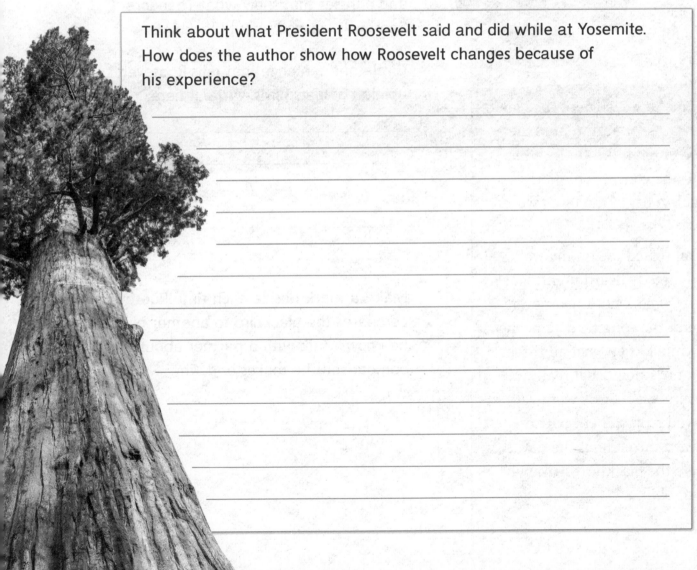

_____

_____

_____

_____

_____

_____

_____

_____

_____

_____

_____

Quick Tip

Use these sentence starters to organize your text evidence.

- *The author tells about Roosevelt's trip by . . .*

- *The dialogue and illustrations help me to . . .*

- *This helps me understand that Roosevelt . . .*

Self-Selected Reading

Choose a text to read independently. Reading for a sustained period of time will help you develop a stronger connection to stories and topics you are interested in. Fill in your writer's notebook with the title, author, and genre. Record your purpose for reading. For example, you can tell why you chose the text and what you hope to find out by reading it.

haveseen/Shutterstock.com

A Walk with Teddy

Literature Anthology:
pages 28–31

1   "We left London on the morning of June 9…Getting off the train at Basingstoke, we drove to the pretty, smiling valley of the Itchen. Here we tramped for three or four hours, then again drove, this time to the edge of the New Forest, where we first took tea at an inn, and then tramped through the forest to an inn on its other side, at Brockenhurst. At the conclusion of our walk my companion made a list of the birds we had seen…

2   The bird that most impressed me on my walk was the blackbird. I had already heard nightingales in abundance near Lake Como… but I had never heard either the blackbird, the song thrush, or the blackcap warbler; and while I knew that all three were good singers, I did not know what really beautiful singers they were. Blackbirds were very abundant, and they played a prominent part in the chorus which we heard throughout the day… In its habits and manners the blackbird strikingly resembles our American robin… "

Reread paragraphs 1 and 2. **Underline** words and phrases that show what Theodore Roosevelt learned about blackbirds.

Circle one sentence that tells Roosevelt's opinion of blackbirds. Write it here:

_____

_____

_____

_____

_____

Make a mark beside each time Roosevelt compares the blackbird to another bird he knows. Talk with a partner about the comparisons he makes and why.

Andrew Howe/Photodisc/Getty Images

A Man of Action

1   Roosevelt realized that seeing and hearing these birds in the wild gave him more information than any book. He could see the birds in action. He could hear their calls to each other. His experience revealed much about the birds of the country.

2   Roosevelt continued to travel throughout his life. He took every opportunity to study animals in the wild. But his travels also showed him that habitats needed to be protected. In his years as president, Roosevelt worked to preserve land. He established 150 national forests, 4 national parks, and 51 bird reservations. These sites continue to protect the nation's wildlife.

Reread paragraph 1. **Circle** all the ways that Roosevelt gained information about birds.

Draw a box around what his experience taught him.

COLLABORATE

Reread paragraph 2. Look at the photograph and the caption. **Underline** the words that help you see how Roosevelt took action as president.

Talk with a partner about why "A Man of Action" is a good title for this section. Use your annotations and the photograph to support your response.

_____

_____

_____

_____

Roosevelt declared Crater Lake a national park. This lake is the deepest lake in the United States. It has a depth of 1,943 feet.

? **How do the excerpts, photograph, and caption help you understand that Roosevelt's trip to England had a lasting impact on him?**

COLLABORATE

Talk About It Reread the excerpt on page 19 and look at the photograph. Talk with a partner about the things Roosevelt did after his trip to England.

Cite Text Evidence Give examples of information about Roosevelt's experiences with nature. Use the web to record text evidence.

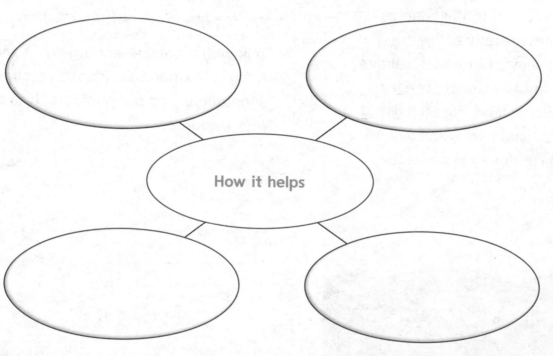

How it helps

Write I know Roosevelt's trip had an impact on his life because

_____

_____

_____

Newman Mark/Prisma by Dukas Presseagentur GmbH/Alamy Stock Photo

Point of View

Point of view refers to whom is telling the story. In an autobiography, the author uses first-person point of view to tell about his or her own experience. In a third-person point of view, the author tells about someone else's experience.

🔍 FIND TEXT EVIDENCE

"A Walk with Teddy" on pages 18–19 tells the story of a bird walk Theodore Roosevelt took in England. The author includes Roosevelt's first-person account of the walk, and then switches to a third-person point of view to tell how this walk was important to Roosevelt.

"The bird that most impressed me on my walk was the blackbird."	Roosevelt realized that seeing and hearing these birds in the wild gave him more information than any book.

 Your Turn Reread the rest of the second paragraph on page 18 and the first paragraph on page 19.

- Choose a sentence from page 19 and rewrite it from the first-person point of view of Roosevelt. _____

  _____

- Why do you think the author included Roosevelt's own words? _____

  _____

Authors may quote someone who experienced an event, and then interpret, or explain, the event for readers. Think about how you might use this technique in your own writing.

Text Connections

Quick Tip

Use details in the photograph to help you experience nature. Then think about the authors' messages about nature.

? How do the photographer and the authors of *Camping with the President* and "A Walk with Teddy" help you experience nature and change the way you think about it?

Talk About It Look at the photograph and read the caption. Talk with a partner about how it makes you feel and why.

Cite Text Evidence **Underline** the cause and effect of the Bald Eagle Protection Act noted in the caption. **Circle** three details in the photo that show how powerful and strong this bald eagle is. Think about how the authors use words and phrases to paint pictures of nature in the selections you read this week.

Write The photographer and authors help me experience nature by _____

_____

_____

_____

_____

_____

_____

In 1940, the Bald Eagle Protection Act was passed to prevent bald eagles from going extinct. In 2007, the bird was no longer threatened because its population had greatly recovered.

Present Your Work

COLLABORATE

Discuss how you will present your promotional map of a national park. Use the Presenting Checklist as you practice your presentation. Discuss the sentence starters below and write your answers.

In my research about a national park, I discovered _____

_____

_____

_____

If I visited this park, I would like to see _____

_____

_____

_____

Quick Tip

Have a member of your group sit in the back of the room or presentation space. During your rehearsal, have the member let you know if he or she can see and hear everything. Adjust the volume of your voice as needed.

✓ Presenting Checklist

☐ Rehearse your presentation.

☐ When presenting your map, point out the park's special features. Tell why people should visit the park.

☐ Present your information in a logical, organized sequence. Use conventions of language such as speaking in complete sentences.

☐ Make sure that your audience can see your map.

☐ Make eye contact with your audience.

William Silver/Shutterstock.com

Literature Anthology:
pages 28–31

Expert Model

Features of a Personal Narrative

A personal narrative is a piece of nonfiction writing that tells a story from the author's life. A personal narrative

- is told from the first-person point of view and expresses the writer's thoughts and feelings about an experience

- follows a logical sequence of events

- uses descriptive details to help the reader understand the experience

Analyze an Expert Model Studying a personal narrative will help you learn how to write a personal narrative of your own. **Reread** page 29, a segment of Theodore Roosevelt's autobiography, in the **Literature Anthology**. Write your answers to the questions below.

What details from the text tell you that this section of "A Walk with

Teddy" is a personal narrative? _____

_____

Look at the first paragraph on page 29. List three examples of words or phrases the author uses to show the sequence of events.

1 _____

2 _____

3 _____

Word Wise

In the first paragraph on page 29, Roosevelt says, "we drove to the pretty, smiling valley . . ." Authors sometimes use human behaviors to describe non-human things. This is called personification. Personification is a type of figurative language. It gives human qualities to an animal or object to help create an image in the reader's mind.

Plan: Choose Your Topic

Freewrite Think about important events in your life that you remember clearly. These might be events such as a class trip or a challange you completed. Quickly write your ideas below without stopping. Then discuss your ideas with a partner.

_____

_____

_____

Writing Prompt Choose one of your ideas that you want to expand into a personal narrative.

I will write my personal narrative about _____

Purpose and Audience Think about who will read or hear your narrative. Will your purpose be to persuade, inform, or entertain them? Then think about the language you will use to write your narrative.

My purpose is to _____

My audience will be _____

I will use _____ language when I write my personal narrative.

Plan Think about what you want your readers to learn about the experience. Ask yourself questions and answer them in your writer's notebook. Questions to ask might include: _Why was the experience important? What did I learn from it? How do I feel about it?_ Include specfic facts and details in your answers.

Plan: Sequence

Sequence of Events Once you have decided on your topic, you will need to plan the sequence, or order, of events in your personal narrative. The sequence of your narrative will help readers understand what happened and why. To make sure you cover everything, answer these questions:

• Am I telling the events in the order that makes the most logical sense?

• How, when, and where does this event begin?

• Have I used signal words and transition words such as *first, earlier, then, next, after, before, later, meanwhile,* and *last* to show the sequence from beginning to end and how events are connected?

List two things you will tell about in the sequence of your narrative.

1_____

_____

2_____

_____

Graphic Organizer In your writer's notebook, make a Sequence of Events map to plan your writing. Fill in the boxes with the main events of your personal narrative in order. Include only the most important details in the chart.

Quick Tip

Think about the order in which things happened to you. Write or draw what happened first, next, and so on. Use these sentence starters to help you.

The story's introduction will include . . .

Then I will tell about . . .

I will end by . . .

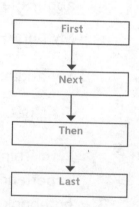

Draft

Description Writers of personal narratives use vivid, descriptive language to show events. They use words and phrases that allow readers to visualize the experience and understand the writer's thoughts and feelings about it. In the sentence below from "A Life in the Woods," Thoreau describes what he sees and feels.

> At length he uttered one of those prolonged howls, as if calling on the god of the loons to aid him, and immediately there came a wind from the east and rippled the surface, and filled the whole air with misty rain, and I was impressed.

Now use the above excerpt as a model to write a paragraph that could be a part of your personal narrative. Think carefully about your descriptions.

_____

_____

_____

_____

_____

Word Wise

To help you come up with descriptive words, close your eyes and think about the experience you are describing. Use words that describe what you saw, heard, smelled, tasted and felt. You can also use a thesaurus to help you find an appropriate descriptive word.

 Write a Draft Use your Sequence of Events map to help you write your draft in your writer's notebook. Don't forget to use signal and transition words to help your audience understand the order in which things happen. Include plenty of descriptive details that will help your readers understand your experience.

Revise

Strong Conclusions An effective personal narrative has a strong conclusion that gives a sense of closure, or ending. Combining ideas may make a conclusion stronger by helping readers focus on the experiences that are most important to the writer. Read the paragraph below. Then revise the last four sentences to make a stronger conclusion.

> Last fall I decided to try out for the school musical. Everyone trying out had to memorize a character's speech for the audition. I was afraid I would forget the words and embarrass myself, so I practiced every night for a week. Finally, it was time for the audition. I went out on the big empty stage and looked at the audience. I said my lines well, and then I heard clapping because I was good at it. I knew I got the part. I smiled. I was happy.

_____

_____

_____

_____

Word wise

The ideas in your conclusion should be coherent, or easy to follow. *Finally, it was time for the audition* is more coherent than *After a while, it was time for the audition, at last.* Combining the ideas of "after a while" and "at last" by using "finally" makes the sentence easier to understand.

Revision Revise your draft, and check that your conclusion is strong. Make sure it shows why the experience was important to you.

asiseeit/E+/Getty Images

Peer Conferences

COLLABORATE

Review a Draft Listen carefully as a partner reads his or her work aloud. Take notes about what you liked and what was difficult to follow. Begin by telling what you liked about the draft. Ask questions that will help the writer think more about the writing. Make suggestions that you think will make the writing stronger. Use these sentence starters.

I enjoyed this part of your draft because . . .

You might improve this description by . . .

I have a question about . . .

This part is unclear to me. Can you explain why . . . ?

Partner Feedback After your partner gives you feedback on your draft, write one of the suggestions that you will use in your revision. Refer to the rubric on page 31 as you give feedback.

Based on my partner's feedback, I will _____

_____

_____

After you finish giving each other feedback, reflect on the peer conference. What was helpful? What might you do differently next time?

Revision As you revise your draft, use the Revising Checklist to help you figure out what text you may need to move, elaborate on, or delete.

Remember to use the rubric on page 31 to help you with your revision.

✔ Revising Checklist

- ☐ Does my writing fit my purpose and audience?
- ☐ Is my sequence of events clear and logical?
- ☐ Do I have enough descriptive language?
- ☐ Do I have a strong conclusion?

Edit and Proofread

When you **edit** and **proofread** your writing, you look for and correct mistakes in spelling, punctuation, capitalization, and grammar. Reading through a revised draft multiple times can help you make sure you're catching any errors. Use the checklist below to edit your narrative.

Editing Checklist

☐ Do all sentences begin with a capital letter and end with a punctuation mark?

☐ Have I used commas correctly?

☐ Do all of my sentences express a complete thought?

☐ Are proper nouns capitalized?

☐ Are quotation marks used correctly?

☐ Are all words spelled correctly?

Grammar Connections

Personal narratives may include dialogue. Lines of dialogue are set off by quotation marks. Make sure you have used quotation marks correctly in any dialogue you write. Use a comma to separate a phrase, such as *she said*, from the quotation itself. For example: *My sister said, "I think that is a terrific idea!"*

List two mistakes you found as you proofread your narrative.

1 _____

_____

2 _____

_____

Publish, Present, and Evaluate

Publishing When you **publish** your writing, you create a clean, neat final copy that is free of mistakes. As you write your final draft be sure to write legibly in cursive. Check that you are holding your pencil or pen correctly.

Presentation When you are ready to **present** your work, rehearse your presentation. Use the Presenting Checklist to help you.

Evaluate After you publish your writing, use the rubric below to **evaluate** your writing.

What did you do successfully? _____

What needs more work? _____

_____

4	3	2	1
• uses plenty of descriptive language to tell about a personal experience, including thoughts and feelings	• uses some descriptive language to tell about a personal experience, including thoughts and feelings	• tells about a personal experience but lacks descriptive language and includes few thoughts and feelings	• does not share a personal experience and has no descriptive details
• has a logical sequence of events with transitional words to connect events	• has a mostly logical sequence of events with some transitional words to connect events	• sequence of events is not logical with few transitional words to connect events	• does not have a particular sequence of events
• has a strong conclusion that gives a sense of closure	• has a conclusion that may not give a complete sense of closure	• has a weak or abrupt conclusion	• does not have a conclusion

Talk About It

COLLABORATE

From the time we get up in the morning to the time we go to sleep at night, we need things to help us survive. We meet these needs in a variety of ways.

Why is this woman in the rice field? Talk with a partner about what the woman does to get what she needs. How does this connect to your society? What other things does she need to live? Write her needs in the web.

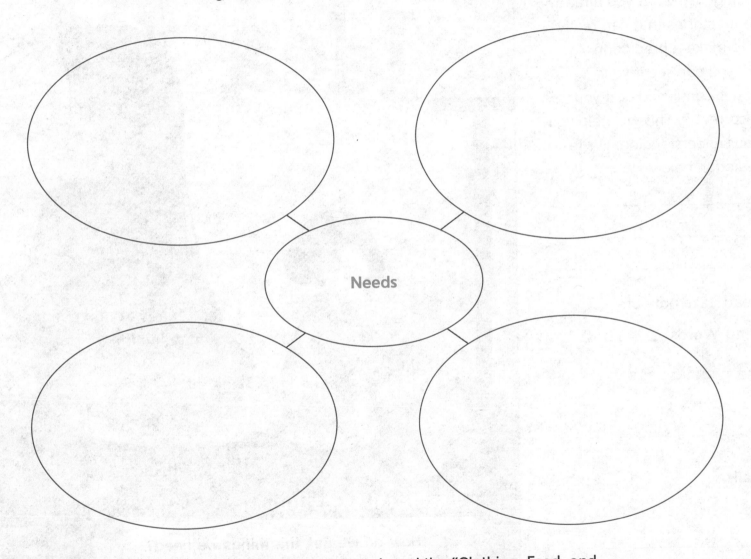

Needs

BLAST BACK!
studysync

Go online to **my.mheducation.com** and read the "Clothing, Food, and Shelter" Blast. Think about the things that people need to survive. How could you help others in society get what they need? Then blast back your response.

TAKE NOTES

Making predictions helps you focus your reading. Use what you already know about stories that can really happen to make a prediction. As you read, you can see if your prediction is confirmed or if you need to correct it. This will help you check your understanding. Write your prediction below.

_____
_____
_____

As you read, take note of:

Interesting Words _____

_____
_____
_____

Key Details _____

_____
_____
_____

A Fresh Idea

Essential Question

How do we get the things we need?

Read about how one girl meets a need in her neighborhood.

One bright Saturday morning, Mali and her mom walked around the neighborhood. That is, her mom walked, but Mali ran, skipped, jumped over puddles, and visited the neighbors' dogs. Mali paused to look at the budding trees on her block. "I can't wait until summer," she said, "especially for Mrs. Fair's great tomatoes at her market stand." She pointed.

Mali's mom stood looking at the empty lot where the market set up every summer weekend. She looked at Mali. "Honey, Mrs. Fair told me last week that she had to close her stand. She's really getting too old to run it anymore."

Mali turned, stared, and put her hands on her hips. "But Mrs. Fair's stand can't close!" she said. "It's the only place in the neighborhood we can buy fresh, delicious tomatoes." Then she added, to show she wasn't being selfish, "Everyone needs fruits and vegetables for a healthy diet."

After they got home, Mali headed out to her backyard swing to think. "If only I could plant a garden," she thought, "but our yard is way too small." Just then, she noticed her neighbor, Mr. Taylor, looking at his daffodils. Mali knew he was thinking about how he had planted those flowers with his wife. This was the first spring since his wife had died, and Mali saw the sadness on his face. Then she had an idea.

FIND TEXT EVIDENCE

Read

Paragraphs 1–3

Reread

In paragraph 1, Mali is happy. In paragraph 3, she is upset. **Draw a box** around what causes Mali's mood to change.

Paragraph 3

Context Clues

Circle the words that help you determine what *diet* means. Write its meaning.

_____

Paragraph 4

Sequence

Underline the character introduced in paragraph 4. Is this before or after Mali thinks about her problem?

_____

Reread

Author's Craft

How does the author help you learn about Mali and Mr. Taylor?

Valerie Decampo

SHARED READ

FIND TEXT EVIDENCE

Read

Paragraphs 1–3

Reread

How can rereading the first three paragraphs help you understand and retell Mali's idea?

_____

_____

_____

_____

_____

_____

Paragraphs 4–6

Sequence

Underline three events that retell important elements of the story.

Reread

Author's Craft

How does the falling action show the changes in Mr. Taylor and Mali's relationship?

Mali cleared her throat, and Mr. Taylor looked up. Mali decided to walk over to the fence. "Hi, Mr. Taylor," she said. He waved, and turned away. "Wait!" Mali cried. Taking a **risk** while she still felt brave, she rushed to gather her thoughts: "Mr. Taylor, Mrs. Fair isn't doing her tomato stand anymore because she's getting old. So I'd like to grow tomatoes. I don't want to get in the way of your flowers, though. I mean, I really like tomatoes."

Suddenly, Mr. Taylor smiled. "Mali, I'm not sure what you're talking about, but you've made me smile. Reasons to smile have been **scarce** lately. What do you want to do?"

As Mr. Taylor listened, an idea came to him. "I still need a place to plant my flowers, but there's room for tomatoes. How about I make you a **loan?** I'll let you use a plot of land in my yard. I'll help you, and when your garden starts to **prosper,** you can repay me with a few tomatoes."

Mali and Mr. Taylor shook hands on this deal. "But first," Mr. Taylor said, "you'll have to make an investment by buying some tomato plants at the nursery."

Mali thought. "Well, I have some **savings** from my allowance, and I was saving to buy a computer game." She paused. "But I'd rather have tomatoes, so let's start right away!"

The next day, Mali bought all the tomato plants she could **afford.** Mr. Taylor taught Mali how to prepare the soil and place the plants. Finally, Mali placed stakes as supports in the ground to help hold the plants up. Mr. Taylor explained, "Once the tomatoes come, the heavy fruit makes the branches bend." Then all they could do was water, pull weeds, and wait.

When the fruit ripened, there were more juicy, red tomatoes than even Mali could have imagined. "There is no way I can eat all these," she realized. On Saturday, Mali and Mr. Taylor carried several crates of ripe tomatoes to the market, and by the day's end they had sold them all. "Not only did I get back the money I invested," said Mali, "but I also made a **profit** of twenty dollars!"

Mr. Taylor said, "Those are also your **wages!** You've earned that money."

Mali beamed and said, "Mr. Taylor, maybe you could sell some of your flowers, and we could run a market stand together!" Mr. Taylor, picturing a garden of zinnias and marigolds, was already looking forward to next summer.

Summarize

Use your notes to orally summarize what happened in the story and to describe the main characters. Talk about whether your prediction from page 34 was confirmed or if it needed correction.

Valerie Decampo

FIND TEXT EVIDENCE

Read

Paragraphs 1–2
Sequence
Underline what happens that changes Mali's original idea of growing tomatoes for herself.

Paragraph 3
Plot
Draw a box around what Mali says to Mr. Taylor in paragraph 3. How does the story end?

_____

_____

Reread

Author's Craft

How does the author help you see how Mr. Taylor's mood has changed?

Fluency

Take turns with a partner reading the last two paragraphs. Talk about how punctuation helped you read with phrasing and expression.

Vocabulary

Use the example sentences to talk with a partner about each word. Then answer the questions.

afford

Jill looked at the price tag to see if she could **afford** to buy the blouse.

Name something you would like to be able to afford.

_____

_____

loan

Lin asked her mom for a **loan** of five dollars.

When have you made a loan to someone?

_____

_____

profit

Jem made a **profit** of five dollars from selling lemonade.

When have you made a profit?

_____

_____

prosper

With enough care, a garden can **prosper**.

What other things help people to prosper?

_____

_____

risk

Firefighters take a great **risk** when they enter a burning building.

In what other jobs do people take a risk?

_____

_____

 Build Your Word List Reread the first paragraph on page 37. Circle the word *imagined*. In your writer's notebook, use a word web to write more forms of the word. For example, write *imaginative*. Use an online or print dictionary to find more words that are related. Write their definitions.

savings

Ray sets aside one dollar a week and puts it into his **savings**.

What would you do with some savings?

_____

_____

_____

scarce

Water can become **scarce** during hot, dry weather.

What is another word or phrase for scarce?

_____

_____

_____

wages

Sam earns **wages** for raking leaves every autumn.

What is a synonym for wages?

_____

_____

_____

Context Clues

Words and phrases in a sentence may help you figure out the meaning of an unfamiliar or multiple-meaning word. Sometimes clues may be in the form of synonyms, words with the same meanings, or antonyms, words with opposite meanings.

🔍 FIND TEXT EVIDENCE

I'm not sure what plot _means in the sentence_ "I'll let you use a plot of land in my yard." _But I can use the phrase "in my yard" with the word "land" to figure out that "plot" means "a piece of ground."_

I'll let you use a plot of land in my yard. I'll help you, and when your garden starts to prosper, you can repay me with a few tomatoes.

Your Turn Use sentence clues to figure out the meanings of the following words from "A Fresh Idea."

stakes, page 36 _____

_____

ripened, page 37 _____

_____

Reread

When you read a story for the first time, you might find that some events or characters' relationships seem unclear. As you read "A Fresh Idea," stop and reread difficult parts of the story to make sure you understand them. Retell the events and analyze, or describe, the characters' relationships to check your understanding of the story.

 FIND TEXT EVIDENCE

You may not be sure how Mali got her idea to grow a garden of her own, with Mr. Taylor's help. Reread the fourth paragraph on page 35.

Page 35

> Just then, she noticed her neighbor, Mr. Taylor, looking at his daffodils. Mali knew he was thinking about how he had planted those flowers with his wife. This was the first spring since his wife had died, and Mali saw the sadness on his face. Then she had an idea.

When I read, I see that Mr. Taylor knows how to plant gardens. He is also sad because his wife died. Mali got her idea after noticing Mr. Taylor's flowers and his sadness.

 Your Turn Reread page 37. Discuss and retell why Mali decides to sell her tomatoes. Also tell what Mr. Taylor's actions show about his relationship with Mali. Remember to use the Reread strategy.

_____

_____

_____

Plot

Realistic fiction is a made-up story that has characters who look and act like real people and often includes dialogue. It takes place in a setting that could be real and has a plot, or story events, that could really happen. A conflict, or problem, is introduced at the beginning of the story. The elements, or parts, of a plot include rising action, climax, falling action, and resolution.

FIND TEXT EVIDENCE

I can tell that "A Fresh Idea" is realistic fiction. Details about the neighborhood show it could be a real place. The characters say and do things that real people might say and do. All the events could really happen.

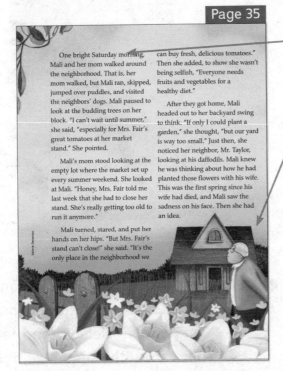

Page 35

One bright Saturday morning, Mali and her mom walked around the neighborhood. That is, her mom walked, but Mali ran, skipped, jumped over puddles, and visited the neighbors' dogs. Mali paused to look at the budding trees on her block. "I can't wait until summer," she said, "especially for Mrs. Fair's great tomatoes at her market stand." She pointed.

Mali's mom stood looking at the empty lot where the market set up every summer weekend. She looked at Mali. "Honey, Mrs. Fair told me last week that she had to close her stand. She's really getting too old to run it anymore."

Mali turned, stared, and put her hands on her hips. "But Mrs. Fair's stand can't close!" she said. "It's the only place in the neighborhood we can buy fresh, delicious tomatoes." Then she added, to show she wasn't being selfish, "Everyone needs fruits and vegetables for a healthy diet."

After they got home, Mali headed out to her backyard swing to think. "If only I could plant a garden," she thought, "but our yard is way too small." Just then, she noticed her neighbor, Mr. Taylor, looking at his daffodils. Mali knew he was thinking about how he had planted those flowers with his wife. This was the first spring since his wife had died, and Mali saw the sadness on his face. Then she had an idea.

Plot

The plot is the sequence of events that make up a story.

Illustrations

Illustrations can give readers visual clues about characters, settings, and events.

COLLABORATE

Your Turn Analyze the plot elements in "Fresh Idea." How does the rising action lead to the climax?_____

_____

_____

_____

Sequence

The sequence is the order in which the **plot events** happen in a story. The sequence of events includes the most important events at the beginning, middle, and end. Sequence also includes when **characters** and **settings** are introduced.

 FIND TEXT EVIDENCE

When I read the paragraphs on page 35 of "A Fresh Idea," I can see the sequence of events that leads to Mali's idea. The beginning of the story introduces Mali, her mom, and their neighborhood. Then we learn about Mali's problem.

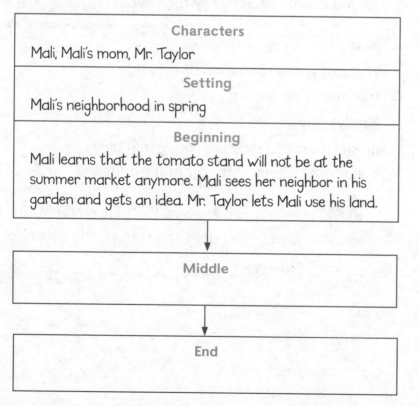

Characters
Mali, Mali's mom, Mr. Taylor

Setting
Mali's neighborhood in spring

Beginning
Mali learns that the tomato stand will not be at the summer market anymore. Mali sees her neighbor in his garden and gets an idea. Mr. Taylor lets Mali use his land.

Middle

End

 Your Turn Reread "A Fresh Idea." List events in the middle and end of the story in your graphic organizer on page 43. Select important details that show the sequence of events.

Characters

Mali, Mali's mom, Mr. Taylor

Setting

Mali's neighborhood in spring

Beginning

Mali learns that the tomato stand will not be at the summer market anymore. Mali sees her neighbor in his garden and gets an idea. Mr. Taylor lets Mali use his land.

Middle

End

Respond to Reading

Discuss the prompt below. Think about how the author developed the relationship between characters in "A Fresh Idea." Use your notes and graphic organizer.

How does the author show how the characters help each other to solve their problems?

_____

_____

_____

_____

_____

_____

_____

_____

_____

_____

_____

_____

_____

Quick Tip

Use these sentence starters to discuss the text and to organize ideas.

- In "A Fresh Idea," Mali finds out . . .
- Mali asks Mr. Taylor . . .
- Mr. Taylor listens to Mali and . . .

Grammar Connections

As you write your response, think about how you can merge your sentences by combining ideas into compound sentences using words such as *and, but, or,* or *so.* For example:

Mali wants to plant a garden.

Mali's yard is too small.

These sentences can be combined.

Mali wants to plant a garden, but her yard is too small.

Evaluate Sources

Evaluate sources for a research project to make sure they are reliable, or trusted for information. For example, primary and secondary sources from a museum or print encyclopedias are credible. Generate and answer questions such as these about your resources.

- Is the website, article, or video from a trusted, reliable source?
- Is the source current?
- Does the source seem exaggerated or appear incomplete?

What might you do to answer questions you have about the information in a resource?

_____

_____

 Tech Tip

Skim, read quickly, and scan, search quickly, a multimodal or digital text to look for information you need. A multimodal text uses words, pictures, or videos together to give information. A digital text, read on a computer, may have links you can click on for more information.

History of Farming Project With a partner or group, plan a research project that compares and contrasts the changes in the United States' farming industry over the past decades. Select a genre, such as a composition with graphic features or an argument explaining the most effective methods of farming. Keep your audience in mind when you choose your genre. Map your ideas in a graphic organizer and include facts such as these

- tools and machinery
- planting and harvesting
- kinds of crops

Then develop your presentation and write, revise, and edit your information. After you finish, you will present your work to the class.

One Hen

 How does the author help you understand the future Kojo dreams about?

Literature Anthology:
pages 32-45

 Talk About It Reread the last five paragraphs on **Literature Anthology** page 34. Turn to your partner and talk about what Kojo's plans are.

Cite Text Evidence What words and phrases tell about Kojo's plan for the future? Write text evidence and tell why it's important to the story.

Text Evidence	Why It's Important

 Evaluate Information

One Hen takes place in Ghana. Ghana is located in West Africa, where there are many farming villages. How does the cultural setting affect Kojo?

Write The author describes Kojo's dreams because _____

_____

_____

How does the author organize the events in the story to help you understand how one hen impacts Kojo's life?

 Talk About It Reread **Literature Anthology** page 40. Turn to your partner and retell what is happening in Kojo's life.

Cite Text Evidence How is each event in Kojo's life connected to the one before it? Write text evidence.

Quick Tip

Retelling can help you better understand the story. When you retell, use text evidence, such as specific details, to help you maintain the story's meaning and the logical order of events.

```
┌──────────────────────────┐
│                          │
└──────────────────────────┘
            ↓
┌──────────────────────────┐
│                          │
└──────────────────────────┘
            ↓
┌──────────────────────────┐
│                          │
└──────────────────────────┘
            ↓
┌──────────────────────────┐
│                          │
└──────────────────────────┘
```

Write The author helps me understand how one hen impacts Kojo's life by _____

_____

_____

_____

? **How do you know that Kojo's dream will continue to come true?**

Quick Tip

A cause is the reason that something happens. The effect is the result. Use these sentence starters to talk about causes and effects.

- *The effect is . . .*
- *That happened because . . .*

COLLABORATE

Talk About It Reread **Literature Anthology** page 43. Talk with a partner about why Kojo gives Adika a loan.

Cite Text Evidence What clue tells you that Kojo is always thinking about the future? Use the chart to record text evidence.

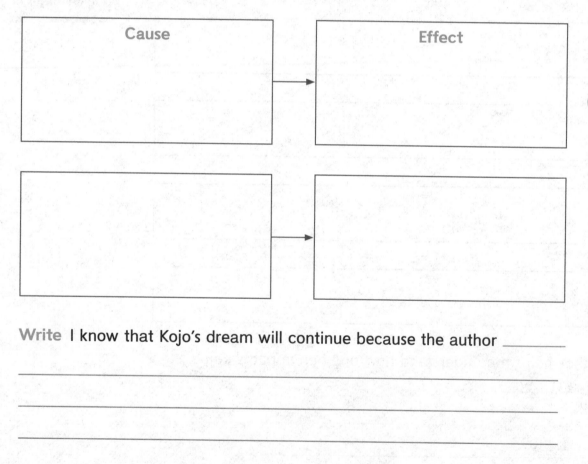

Cause	Effect

Make Inferences

An inference is a decision you make about what you read based on the text evidence. Think about what you know about Kojo. What inference can you make about why Kojo thinks positively about the future?

Write I know that Kojo's dream will continue because the author _____

_____

_____

_____

Respond to Reading

COLLABORATE

Discuss the prompt below. Recall the details of the events that happen to Kojo to inform your answer. Use your notes and graphic organizer.

How does the author help you understand how Kojo changes and how he changes the lives of so many people?

_____

_____

_____

_____

_____

_____

_____

_____

_____

_____

_____

_____

Eureka/Alamy Stock Photo

Quick Tip

Use these sentence starters to talk about and organize your text evidence.

- *Katie Smith Milway starts and ends the story . . .*

- *She uses cause and effect to . . .*

- *This helps me understand . . .*

Self-Selected Reading

Choose a text and fill in your writer's notebook with the title, author, and genre. Include a personal response to the text in your writer's notebook. You make a personal connection when the text reminds you of something in your life or makes you feel a certain way. To help you choose a text, read the first page and see if it interests you.

Reading Between the Dots

Literature Anthology:
pages 48–51

1   "Brittany, you have so many library books in this house, it isn't funny!" my grandmother yelled from the living room. You would think 30 library books in the house wouldn't be a pain, right? Wrong. That's because these books were Braille books. For those of you who don't know, Braille is a raised-dot code, invented by Louis Braille, that blind or visually disabled individuals read using their fingers. Braille takes up a lot of room on a page. One book in print can be many volumes in Braille.

2   My work as a library volunteer started in the summer of 2008. The Baltimore public school system required all of its students to do community service before graduation. I decided to volunteer at my state library for the blind and physically handicapped.

3   On my first day, I made six Braille copies of a booklet. No, I didn't have to make all of those bumps by hand! Like other Braille documents and books, the booklet was typed on a computer. A special program converted the print file into a Braille file. Then a machine called a Braille embosser was hooked up to a computer and made six copies of the booklet in a matter of minutes.

Reread paragraph 1. **Underline** the sentence that explains what Braille is.

Reread paragraph 2. **Draw a box** around the text that explains why Brittany volunteered at the library.

COLLABORATE

Reread paragraph 3. Talk with a partner about how the author used a machine to make copies instead of doing it by hand. Write the text evidence here:

_____

_____

_____

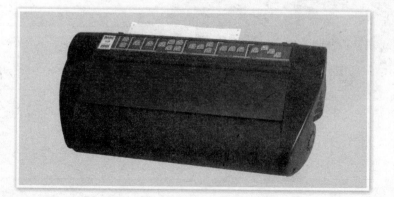

Louis Braille

1 Louis Braille was born in France in 1809. He lost his vision at the age of three after a terrible accident. During his childhood, Braille attended the National Institute for Blind Youth in Paris. While there, he thought of ways to make reading easier for blind people. The method at that time was to read raised letters. But most blind people were unable to do this with much success.

2 Braille came up with his idea for using raised dots instead after learning about a French officer in Napoleon's army who used a similar idea to help his soldiers communicate in the dark without making noise. By 1824, Braille had invented his raised dot code to help blind people read more efficiently. Over the years he improved his system, and it is still widely used today.

Reread paragraph 1. **Draw a box** around the text that tells how blind people used to read. Write it here:

_____

_____

_____

Reread paragraph 2. **Underline** the text that tells where Braille got his idea for using raised dots.

COLLABORATE

Talk with a partner about why Braille's system is still successful. **Circle** the text evidence that tells why it is still used today.

BRAILLE ALPHABET
ENGLISH version

ALPHABET:

A B C D E F G H I J

K L M N O P Q R S T

U V W X Y Z   CH SH TH

PUNCTUATION:

? ! . -

, ; : /

" - ()

NUMBERS:

1 2 3 4 5 6 7 8 9 0

capital follows   number follows   decimal point

? How does the title "Reading Between the Dots" relate to the personal narrative?

Talk About It Reread the paragraphs on **Literature Anthology** pages 50 and 51. Talk with a partner about how Braille books are made.

Cite Text Evidence What are some details about Braille's system? How is Braille used? Use the chart to record text evidence.

```
┌────────────────────────────────────────┐
│                 Detail                   │
└────────────────────────────────────────┘
                    │
                    ▼
┌────────────────────────────────────────┐
│                 Detail                   │
└────────────────────────────────────────┘
                    │
                    ▼
┌────────────────────────────────────────┐
│                 Detail                   │
└────────────────────────────────────────┘
                    │
                    ▼
┌────────────────────────────────────────┐
│               Conclusion                 │
└────────────────────────────────────────┘
```

Write The title "Reading Between the Dots" relates to the personal narrative because _____

_____

Quick Tip

A conclusion is a decision you reach based on details and evidence. You can draw a conclusion about the texts you read. For example:

Dentists recommend you brush your teeth.

Dentists also suggest you floss every day.

From these details, you can conclude that dentists feel that taking care of your teeth every day is important.

Text Structure

A personal narrative describes events the author experienced. The narrative may be structured by a logical order of events or their order of importance. A personal narrative may start with an anecdote, or a brief account of some incident, to grab the reader's attention. The anecdote may entertain, inform, persuade, or inspire the reader.

 FIND TEXT EVIDENCE

Read page 50 of "Reading Between the Dots." The first paragraph is an anecdote. Below is the beginning of the anecdote.

> "Brittany, you have so many library books in this house, it isn't funny!" my grandmother yelled from the living room. You would think 30 library books in the house wouldn't be a pain, right?

 Your Turn Reread the first two paragraphs on page 50.

- How does the author structure the text?

  _____

  _____

- What is the author's purpose for using an anecdote to begin her personal narrative? _____

  _____

  _____

Readers to Writers

Structuring a personal narrative in a logical order will help readers understand your experience. Focusing on parts of the experience in more detail will show readers what you think is most important. You may start a personal narrative with an anecdote.

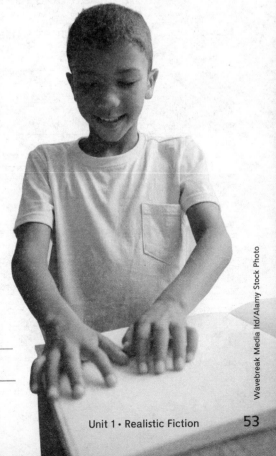

Text Connections

? How is the way the poet uses cause and effect in "Try Again" similar to the way the authors use cause and effect in *One Hen* and "Reading Between the Dots"?

Talk About It Read the poem. Talk with a partner about what the poet wants you to know and how the poem is organized.

Cite Text Evidence Reread the poem. **Circle** the phrase the poet repeats. **Underline** words and phrases that tell what would happen if you follow the poet's advice. This is the effect. **Draw a box** around the cause. Compare how the authors use cause and effect in the selections you read this week.

Write The poet's use of cause and effect is similar to _____

_____

_____

_____

_____

_____

_____

_____

_____

> **Quick Tip**
>
> When you compare ideas, you show how they are the same. To help you compare ideas in the readings, think about how one event causes another to happen in *One Hen* and "Reading Between the Dots." Then do the same for "Try Again."

Try Again

If you find your task is hard,
  Try again;
Time will bring you your reward,
  Try again.
All that other folks can do,
With your patience should not you?
Only keep this rule in view—
  Try again.

— Anonymous

Present Your Work

 COLLABORATE

Discuss how you will present your information about the United States' farming industry from a point in the past to the present. Use the Presenting Checklist as you practice your presentation. Discuss the sentence starters below and write your answers.

Quick Tip

When you speak, you need to use correct grammar. This will help you communicate your ideas effectively. For example, speak in complete sentences and make sure your verbs agree with your subjects.

In my research about the farming industry, I understood its economic impact to be _____

_____

_____

I think the greatest changes are in _____

_____

_____

_____

✔ Presenting Checklist

☐ Rehearse your presentation with your partner or group.

☐ Present your information in a logical, organized sequence. Speak in complete sentences.

☐ Follow the conventions of language, including using correct grammar.

☐ Make sure that your audience can see any graphic features clearly.

☐ Allow time for your audience to ask relevant questions.

Claudia Harms-Warlies/Shutterstock.com

Essential Question

What are the positive and negative effects of new technology?

Look at the photo. It shows a bionic, or artificial, hand. Electronics and new technology give the hand the ability to do almost any everyday task. The hand can pick up small objects, type, carry bags, and hold a ball. Talk with a partner about some positive effects of using a bionic hand. Write your ideas in the web.

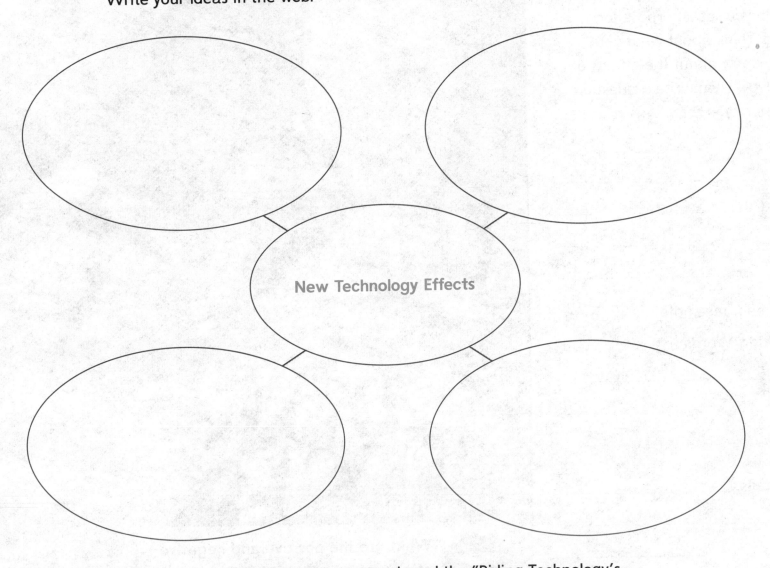

New Technology Effects

 Go online to **my.mheducation.com** and read the "Riding Technology's Rollercoaster" Blast. Think about your experiences with technology. How would you describe them? Then blast back your response.

TAKE NOTES

Asking questions before you read can help you set a purpose for reading. Think about what you already know about the effects of technology. Then write a question here before you read.

_____

_____

_____

_____

_____

As you read, take note of:

Interesting Words _____

_____

_____

_____

Key Details _____

_____

_____

_____

_____

Essential Question

? What are the positive and negative effects of new technology?

Read two different viewpoints about how technology affects kids.

JGI Jamie Grill/Blend Images/Getty Images

Are Electronic Devices Good for Us?

Plugged In

Kids need to spend time using electronic devices.

Do you love to surf the Internet, listen to music, text, and talk on a cell phone? You are not alone. A recent study has some surprising news: Kids in the United States between the ages of 8 and 18 spend seven and a half hours a day on electronic devices. These include computers, smart phones, and video games. Some adults try to **advance** the idea that these devices waste kids' time. However, some research surveys say this idea is inaccurate. In fact, the **data** show that technology can benefit kids.

Critics say that kids who stare at computers and TVs all day do not get enough exercise. The facts stand in **counterpoint** to this belief. One study compared kids who use media a lot to those who do not.

The "heavy" media users actually spent more time in physical activity than "light" media users.

One study by the National Institutes of Health says that action video games may help increase kids' visual attention. In addition, using interactive media can give kids good structure for learning. It can also help them learn to switch tasks effectively. Kids also need to use the Web to **access** information. Many argue that learning to use the Web responsibly sharpens kids' **reasoning** abilities.

Today's world is wired, and not just for fun. The jobs of the future depend on kids who plug in!

A Source of News for Teens

For the latest news, teens used to rely on newspapers, television, and magazines. See how many teens now get their news online.

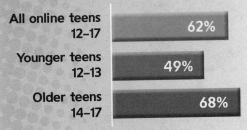

All online teens 12–17	62%
Younger teens 12–13	49%
Older teens 14–17	68%

FIND TEXT EVIDENCE

Read

Paragraph 1

Author's Point of View

Circle the author's claim about electronic devices.
Underline the sentence that is opposite of the author's claim. How does the author use a fact against this opposite claim?

_____

_____

Paragraphs 2–4

Reread

Draw a box around the supporting evidence about visual attention that supports the author's claim.

Reread

Author's Craft

Why did the author include the sidebar graph "A Source of News for Teens"?

FIND TEXT EVIDENCE

Read

Paragraphs 1–2

Author's Point of View

Underline the author's claim about electronic media. What is the author's opinion in the second paragraph?

_____

_____

Graphs

Draw a box around the pie graph that shows which media users get the best grades.

Synthesize Information

What conclusion can you draw about media use?

_____

_____

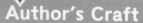
Reread

 Author's Craft

How does the author support his or her argument?

Tuned Out

Electronic media is harming kids.

Are kids tuning out by tuning in to electronic devices? An alarming report states that electronic media use has continued to grow over the past decade, aided by the increase in mobile phone use among teenagers. About 25 percent of teenagers consider themselves "constantly connected" to the Internet. Nearly 6 out of 10 kids get their first cell phone between the ages of 10–11. Are these devices harmless or hurtful to the well-being of young people? A close **analysis** of several studies shows that there are plenty of disadvantages to these devices.

The Internet is supposed to be a great tool for learning. Do kids who love computers do better in the classroom? To **cite** one report, access to electronic devices does not automatically bring high marks in school. See the graphs below.

The Effect of Media Use on Grades

These pie graphs show how the use of media affects grades.

Heavy Media Users

51% Good grades

47% Fair/poor grades

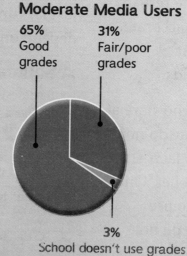

Moderate Media Users

65% Good grades

31% Fair/poor grades

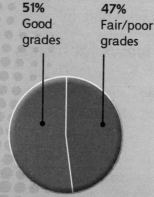

3% School doesn't use grades

Light Media Users

60% Good grades

23% Fair/poor grades

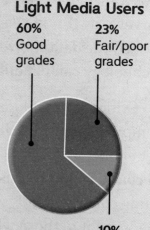

10% School doesn't use grades

The effects of using electronic devices on kids will continue to be studied. These devices seem to be here to stay.

Some argue that the devices get kids involved and help them make friends. Claims like these are incorrect. A study done by the Pew Research Center discusses teenagers' use of online social networks. Teens use social media to keep in touch with friends they already have, not to make new ones. In addition, trying to meet people online can be dangerous.

There are other serious **drawbacks** to new technology. One issue is multitasking, or trying to do many tasks at the same time. Is it possible to do more than one task at a time well? Some studies say kids' thinking improves when they do several tasks at once. Still, experts point out that much more research needs to be done on this.

New electronic devices hit stores every year. Kids should know that there is more to life than what they see on a screen.

Summarize

Use your notes, the graphs, and the answer to your question to write two summary sentences for each part of "Are Electronic Devices Good for Us?"

FIND TEXT EVIDENCE

Read

Paragraph 1

Greek and Latin Prefixes

The prefix *in-* sometimes means "not." What does the word *incorrect* mean?

Paragraph 2

Reread

Draw a box around what experts think about multitasking.

Paragraph 3

Author's Point of View

Underline the author's opinion in the last paragraph.
Who was the intended audience for this text?

Reread

Author's Craft

How does the author address and refute any counterargument?

Thomas Barwick/Iconica/Getty Images

Vocabulary

Use the example sentences to talk with a partner about each word. Then answer the questions.

access

Brad had to use a key to **access** the locked room.

How do you access information on a computer?

_____

_____

advance

Many people have marched to **advance** people's rights.

What would you do to advance a cause you believed in?

_____

_____

Build Your Word List Pick a word you found interesting in the selection you read. Look up the definition and the word's origin, the language the word comes from, in a print or online dictionary. Write the word and its definition and origin in your writer's notebook.

analysis

Karina used a magnifying glass to make a careful **analysis** of a seashell.

How do you do an analysis of information for a report?

_____

_____

cite

When doing research, it is important to identify and **cite** sources of information.

What sources might you cite when writing a report about a country?

_____

_____

counterpoint

One critic's positive review was in **counterpoint** to another's bad review.

What opinion have you had in counterpoint to that of a friend?

_____

_____

data

The students gathered **data** as they measured the growing plants' heights.

What data would you need to write a weather report?

_____

_____

_____

drawbacks

Fewer seats and a small trunk are **drawbacks** of a small car.

What are some drawbacks to going on a hike without the right equipment?

_____

_____

_____

reasoning

James used his **reasoning** skills before deciding on his next chess move.

What other situations require good reasoning?

_____

_____

_____

Greek and Latin Prefixes

Prefixes are added to the beginning of a word that change the word's meaning. Prefixes that come from ancient Greek and Latin, such as *dis-, in-, tele-,* and *multi-,* are common in many English words. Prefixes can help you figure out an unfamiliar word's meaning.

FIND TEXT EVIDENCE

On page 60 of "Tuned Out," I can use prefixes to figure out the meaning of disadvantages. Dis- *means "opposite."* Advantages *means "qualities that help."* Disadvantages *must mean "harmful qualities."*

> A close analysis of several studies shows that there are plenty of disadvantages to these devices.

Your Turn Use Greek and Latin prefixes to define words from "Tuned Out."

Greek prefix: *tele-* = at a distance

television, *page 60* _____

_____

Latin prefix: *multi-* = many

multitasking, *page 61* _____

Reread

Rereading a text—including opening and closing paragraphs—can help clarify points an author makes. It can help you monitor your comprehension of how ideas are presented and supported by an author. Rereading can also lead you to answer questions when your understanding of the text breaks down.

 FIND TEXT EVIDENCE

When I reread the end of the opening paragraphs of "Plugged In" on page 59 and "Tuned Out" on page 60, I can better understand what the different authors will be writing about.

> Pages 59 and 60
>
> **Plugged In**
> In fact, the **data** show that technology can benefit kids.
>
> **Tuned Out**
> A close **analysis** of several studies show that there are plenty of disadvantages to these devices.

The author of "Plugged In" says technology can benefit kids. The author of "Tuned Out" discusses disadvantages of technology. Rereading helps me see different ideas the authors are making.

 Your Turn Reread the conclusions of "Plugged In" and "Tuned Out." How are they similar or different? _____

_____

_____

Headings and Graphs

"Plugged In" and "Tuned Out" are examples of argumentative text. Both include reasons and evidence that support a claim. Authors of argumentative texts may address a counterargument, or opposite claim, and use facts to say why it may be incorrect. Print and graphic features such as headings and graphs may add support for an argument.

Quick Tip

When you look at a bar graph, read the title first. Then read the other main features, such as captions and labels. Next, look at the bars and compare the sizes. Finally, summarize the information shown by the graph.

🔍 FIND TEXT EVIDENCE

I can tell that "Plugged In" on page 59 is argumentative text. The opening paragraph clearly states an argument. The second paragraph cites a study that supports the author's opinion. A graph adds more support.

Page 59

Are Electronic Devices Good for Us?

Plugged In

Kids need to spend time using electronic devices.

Do you love to surf the Internet, listen to music, text, and talk on a cell phone? You are not alone. A recent study has some surprising news: Kids in the United States between the ages of 8 and 18 spend seven and a half hours a day on electronic devices. These include computers, smart phones, and video games. Some adults try to advance the idea that these devices waste kids' time. However, some research surveys say this idea is inaccurate. In fact, the data show that technology can benefit kids.

Critics say that kids who stare at computers and TVs all day do not get enough exercise. The facts stand in counterpoint to this belief. One study compared kids who use media a lot to those who do not.

The "heavy" media users actually spent more time in physical activity than "light" media users.

One study by the National Institutes of Health says that action video games may help increase kids' visual attention. In addition, using interactive media can give kids good structure for learning. It can also help them learn to switch tasks effectively. Kids also need to use the Web to access information. Many argue that learning to use the Web responsibly sharpens kids' reasoning abilities.

Today's world is wired, and not just for fun. The jobs of the future depend on kids who plug in!

A Source of News for Teens
For the latest news, teens used to rely on newspapers, television, and magazines. See how many teens now get their news online.

All online teens 12–17: 62%
Younger teens 12–13: 49%
Older teens 14–17: 68%

Headings

A heading tells what a section of text is mainly about.

Graphs

A graph compares two or more quantities of something. Bars or sections show differences in amount. Labels identify the graph's main features.

COLLABORATE

Your Turn List three parts of the bar graph on page 59 of "Plugged In."

_____

_____

_____

_____

Author's Point of View

When authors argue for or against an idea, they give reasons and evidence to support their points. First, authors identify their intended audience or reader. Then, they identify their claim. They use facts, statements that can be proven, to support the claim. Authors also give their opinions, personal feelings that cannot be proven. Facts and opinions help show readers the **author's point of view**.

🔍 FIND TEXT EVIDENCE

In "Plugged In" on page 59, the author's position is stated in the sentence, "Kids need to spend time using electronic devices." The author supports this claim with evidence about exercise and learning. Finally, the author argues that technology creates the jobs of the future. From these details I can identify the author's point of view.

Details	Author's Point of View
Users get exercise.	The author supports kids using electronic devices.
Help kid's visual attention.	
Helps users with learning.	
These are jobs of the future.	

Your Turn Reread the counterpoint, "Tuned Out," on pages 60 and 61. Find details that support the author's argument and list them in the graphic organizer on page 67. Summarize the details to identify the author's point of view.

JGI Jamie Grill/Blend Images/Getty Images

Details	Author's Point of View

Respond to Reading

Discuss the prompt below. Think about how the authors stated and supported an argument about young people's use of electronic devices. Use your notes and graphic organizer.

Which author do you think has the more convincing argument? Cite text evidence to support your answer.

_____

_____

_____

_____

_____

_____

_____

_____

_____

_____

_____

Quick Tip

Use these sentence starters to paraphrase the text as you discuss and organize ideas.

- In "Plugged In," the author references a study in order to show that . . .

- In contrast, the author of "Tuned Out" believes that . . .

- Each author supports arguments with . . .

Grammar Connections

Check your writing for comma splices. A comma splice is when two independent clauses are combined into one sentence with only a comma. For example, *Teens text too much, they should put their phones down* can be written as *Teens text too much. They should put their phones down.*

Debate

A debate is an organized discussion between two people or teams. Each side takes turns arguing for or against an idea. A debate has rules the sides must follow. A moderator keeps track of time, keeps the debaters on topic, and reminds them to observe the rules.

What do you think is one important rule for a debate? Write it here.

_____

_____

Debate In groups of four, divide into two teams to plan a debate about positive and negative effects of a specific kind of technology. Each team will research the main points for their position on the topic. To prepare for a debate

- research facts that support your argument.
- note your sources so that you can cite them during the debate.
- think about how you will respond to points that may be made by the opposing side.

After you complete the preparations, your group will debate in front of the class. During the debate, you will demonstrate your understanding of the information you have gathered. You can demonstrate understanding by using relevant facts to support your argument and by speaking knowingly about the topic.

Debate Format

- One team presents an argument that supports its position.
- The opposing team states its position.
- Each team then takes turns addressing the other team's arguments.
- Each team summarizes its position and closes with why their position is best.

The list above shows a brief outline for a debate.

The Future of Transportation

? How do you know how the author of "Autos Advance" feels about cars?

*Literature Anthology:
pages 52–55*

Talk About It Reread **Literature Anthology** page 53. Turn to your partner and discuss how the author compares modern cars and public transportation. Describe how the author uses literal language to support his claim.

Cite Text Evidence What words and phrases help you understand the author's point of view? Write text evidence to support the opinion.

Public Transportation	Cars

Write I know how the author feels about cars because the author _____

_____

How do print and graphic features help you understand how the author of "The Rail Way" feels about public transportation?

Talk About It Look at the features on **Literature Anthology** pages 54–55. Talk with your partner about how the features support the author's argument.

Cite Text Evidence What new and persuasive information did you learn by using the features? Write the evidence here.

Headings	Photographs	Captions

Write The author uses features to _____

_____

_____

Respond to Reading

Discuss the prompt below. Apply your knowledge about technology to inform
your answer. Use your notes and graphic organizer.

Think about how the authors present their positions on transportation
technology. How do the authors support their arguments?

_____

_____

_____

_____

_____

_____

_____

_____

_____

_____

Quick Tip

Use these sentence
starters to retell details in
a way that maintains
meaning about the texts
and to cite text evidence.

• *In their arguments, each
author . . .*

• *This helps me
understand that . . .*

Self-Selected Reading

Choose a text to read
independently. Reading for
a longer length of time
without interruption will
help you develop a
stronger connection to
stories and topics. Read the
first two pages. If five or
more words are unfamiliar,
you may decide to pick
another text. Fill in your
writer's notebook with the
title, author, and genre.
Include a personal
response to the text.

narvikk/E+/Getty Images

Getting From Here to There

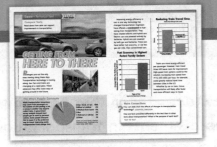

Literature Anthology:
pages 56–57

1. Passengers are not the only ones moving along these days. Transportation technology is moving along, too. Cars and trains are changing at a rapid pace. These advances may offer more ways of getting around in the future.

The Ways People Commute

2. While transportation researchers may count train passengers or the number of cars passing a toll, a survey is another way experts collect data. A government survey analysis showed most people get to work by personal vehicle. Some people interpret this to mean it is the preferred way to travel. Improving public transportation could change that.

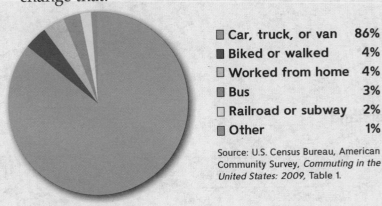

■ Car, truck, or van	86%
■ Biked or walked	4%
☐ Worked from home	4%
■ Bus	3%
☐ Railroad or subway	2%
■ Other	1%

Source: U.S. Census Bureau, American Community Survey, *Commuting in the United States: 2009,* Table 1.

Reread paragraph 1. **Underline** the sentence that shows how the author feels about transportation technology. **Draw a box** around the sentence in paragraph 2 that relates to information in the pie chart.

COLLABORATE

Look at the pie chart. Talk with a partner about what the chart shows. How do you know which is the most popular way people commute? **Circle** the clue.

Draw an arrow to the least popular way people commute.

Chuck Eckert/Alamy Stock Photo

Reread | PAIRED SELECTION

 How does the author help you understand how data can support improvements in transportation?

 Talk About It Reread the excerpt on page 73 and look at the pie chart. Talk with a partner about how the author's use of a chart helps get a point across.

Cite Text Evidence How does the pie chart help make technical information easier to understand? Write evidence in the web below.

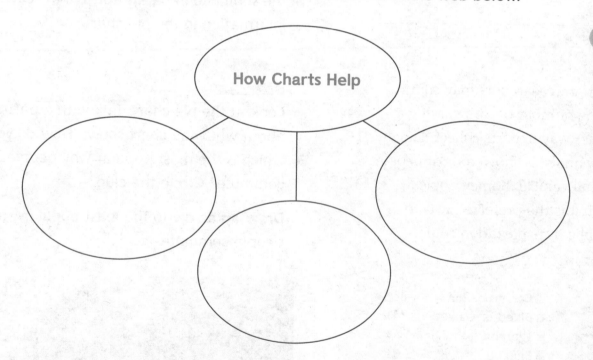

Write The author's use of features helps me understand _____

_____

_____

_____

Author's Purpose

An **author's purpose** is the reason the author writes. This purpose may be to persuade, inform, or entertain. In order to accomplish the purpose, an author thinks about the intended audience or reader. An author may use data when writing to inform or when writing to support a claim.

 FIND TEXT EVIDENCE

On page 73 of "Getting from Here to There," the author expresses support for advances in transportation technology by saying that such advances may provide more transportation choices in the future. Future developments are important to readers.

> Transportation technology is moving along, too. Cars and trains are changing at a rapid pace. These advances may offer more ways of getting around in the future.

 Your Turn Reread the text on page 73 in the section "The Ways People Commute."

- Based on the data, what do some people conclude about personal vehicles? _____

  _____

- Why does the author think the data about cars, trucks, and vans might change? _____

  _____

Stay consistent with your point of view throughout your writing. Use supporting evidence when presenting information. Use convincing facts to support a claim. Also include opposing views and use facts to refute them.

Text Connections

? How is the songwriter's message about transportation similar to the opinions of the authors of *The Future of Transportation* and "Getting from Here to There"?

COLLABORATE

Talk About It Read the song lyrics. Talk with a partner about what the songwriter's message is. Compare what it has in common with the selections you read this week about transportation. When you compare ideas, you look to see how they are similar.

Cite Text Evidence In the song lyrics, **circle** phrases that tell how the writer feels about train travel. **Underline** clues that show why the writer feels this way.

Write The songwriter's message is similar to what the authors think because _____

_____

_____

_____

Quick Tip

Notice how words or ideas are repeated in the lyrics. This repetition can help you understand the message. Then think about how the message compares to the other two texts that you've read.

Down Yonder

Railroad train, railroad train,
  hurry some more;
Put a little steam on just like
  never before.
Hustle on, bustle on, I've got
  the blues,
Yearning for my Swanee
  shore.
Brother if you only knew, you'd
  want to hurry up, too.

— L. Wolfe Gilbert, 1921.

Accuracy and Phrasing

As you read aloud argumentative text, note punctuation in sentences to help you group words into meaningful *phrases*. Also read each word with *accuracy* by pronouncing each word correctly.

Page 59

> **Do you love to surf the Internet, listen to music, text, and talk on a cell phone? You are not alone. A recent study has some surprising news: Kids in the United States between the ages of 8 and 18 spend seven and a half hours a day on electronic devices.**

Pause your reading when you come to commas and use them to group words into meaningful phrases.

Think about how to accurately pronounce words with multiple syllables.

Quick Tip

Try different ways to phrase groups of words and decide what makes the most sense as you read aloud. Practice breaking down and reading multisyllabic words until you can read them with accuracy.

Your Turn Turn back to page 60. Take turns reading aloud the first paragraph with a partner. Think about how you can group words, such as the phrase "An alarming report states that . . ." Plan how you will accurately pronounce technical words and words with multiple syllables.

Afterward, think about how you did. Complete these sentences.

I remembered to _____

_____

Next time, I will _____

_____

WRITING

Expert Model

Literature Anthology
pages 52–55

Features of an Opinion Essay

An opinion essay is a form of argumentative text. It tells about the author's point of view on a topic. An opinion essay

- introduces a clearly stated claim using a consistent voice

- includes facts, details, relevant evidence, and reasons in a logical order to support the claim

- often includes an opposing point of view and then uses facts to refute that point of view

Word Wise

Voice is how authors show their attitude toward a topic through their words. The author's voice can help to express an opinion and persuade the intended audience. In the sentence that starts, *These cool cars,* the word "cool" shows the author's opinion about the cars. The author's voice can engage a reader as if a friend is talking to you.

Analyze an Expert Model Studying argumentative texts will help you learn how to plan and write an opinion essay of your own. **Reread** the first paragraph of *The Future of Transportation* on page 53 in the **Literature Anthology**. Write your answers to the questions below.

What is the author's point of view about how to travel? _____

_____

_____

What words and phrases in the first paragraph contribute to the author's

voice and express the author's opinion? _____

_____

_____

Plan: Choose Your Topic

Freewrite Technological advances have led to advances in social media. Social media helps people stay in touch with family and friends, but some say it is too distracting and time consuming. Talk with a partner about whether or not social media benefits students. Then freewrite a paragraph that states the advantages and disadvantages of social media.

Readers to Writers

You will need to research facts to include in your essay. Paraphrase information by restating details in your own words. Make sure you maintain the meaning and the logical order of the original text. Avoid plagiarism by keeping track of your sources so that you can cite them properly in your essay.

_____

_____

_____

_____

Writing Prompt Decide whether you think social media benefits students or not. Write an opinion essay that presents your point of view. Make sure you include facts and details that support your claim, and address and refute an opposing point of view.

I will write about _____.

Purpose and Audience Think about your purpose for writing.

My purpose is to _____ my readers.

My audience will be _____.

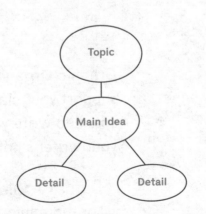

Plan In your writer's notebook, make a Topic and Details web to plan your writing. Write "social media" in the Topic oval. Fill in the Main Idea oval with your point of view.

Plan: Strong Introduction

Write an Effective Introduction You will need to gather information before you begin to write. The introduction is your chance to grab readers' attention with an especially surprising fact or statistic. Your introduction should explain the topic of the essay and clearly state your point of view. As you plan and write your draft, think about these questions:

- Is it clear what topic I will be writing about?

- Is my point of view on the topic clearly stated?

- Am I grabbing my readers' attention with supporting facts and details?

List two details you might include in your introduction.

1 _____

_____

2 _____

_____

Graphic Organizer Once you have decided about information to support your claim, fill in the rest of your web. If you need more space to write your details, use a separate sheet of paper in your writer's notebook.

Digital Tools

For more information on how to write an opinion essay, watch the "Purpose of Opinion Writing" tutorial.
Go to **my.mheducation.com**.

Draft

Relevant Evidence An author uses facts and details as evidence to support his or her point of view when writing an opinion essay. These facts and details must be relevant, or connected, to the topic. In the example below from "Are Electronic Devices Good for Us?" pay attention to the evidence the author includes.

> One study by the National Institutes of Health says that action video games may help increase kids' visual attention. In addition, using interactive media can give kids good structure for learning. It can also help them learn to switch tasks effectively. Kids also need to use the Web to access information. Many argue that learning to use the Web responsibly sharpens kids' reasoning abilities.

Grammar Connections

As you write your draft, make sure that you don't use any run-on sentences. A run-on sentence incorrectly combines two sentences. Break run-on sentences into two sentences or add a comma and a conjunction. For example, *Mona likes to speak on the phone her sister likes to text* can be written as *Mona likes to speak on the phone, but her sister likes to text.*

Now use the paragraph above as a model to write a paragraph for your opinion essay. State a claim and provide relevant evidence from your research to support it.

_____

_____

_____

_____

Write a Draft Use your graphic organizer to help you write your draft in your writer's notebook. Don't forget to write a strong introduction that tells the topic of your essay and states your point of view.

Revise

Logical Order It is important that you present your facts and details in a logical order so that you do not confuse your readers. Read the paragraph below. Then revise it so that the information is presented in a logical order. Add transitions to make your sentences coherent and clear.

> Some adults advance the idea that kids who spend too much time using social media are not using their time well. We need to encourage kids to spend less time on social media. Kids spend too much time using social media, which is not beneficial.

_____

_____

_____

_____

_____

_____

Revision Revise your draft, and check that all of your facts, details, and evidence are presented in the most logical order.

Quick Tip

When you revise your draft, add transition words and phrases to help make your writing coherent, or flow smoothly. For example, introduce a new fact by using *In addition.* Use *however* to make it clear that a sentence is contrasting ideas.

Peer Conferences

Review a Draft Listen carefully as a partner reads his or her work aloud. Take notes about what you liked and what was difficult to follow. Begin by telling what you liked about the draft. Ask questions that will help the writer think more about the writing. Make suggestions that you think will make the writing stronger. Use these sentence starters.

I enjoyed this part of your draft because . . .

You could use more support for the idea that . . .

I have a question about . . .

I am not sure about the order of . . .

Partner Feedback After your partner gives you feedback on your draft, write one of the suggestions that you will use in your revision. Refer to the rubric on page 85 as you give feedback.

Based on my partner's feedback, I will _____

_____

_____

After you finish giving each other feedback, reflect on the peer conference. What was helpful? What might you do differently next time?

Revision As you revise your draft use the Revising Checklist to help you figure out what text you may need to move, elaborate on, or delete. Remember to use the rubric on page 85 to help you with your revision.

✓ Revising Checklist

- ☐ Does my writing fit my purpose and intended audience?
- ☐ Do I have enough relevant evidence to support my claim?
- ☐ Are my facts and details in a logical order?
- ☐ Is my introduction strong enough?
- ☐ Have I used a consistent voice?
- ☐ Are my sentences clear and easy to follow, or do I need to add ideas?

Edit and Proofread

When you **edit** and **proofread** your writing, you look for and correct mistakes in spelling, punctuation, capitalization, and grammar. Reading through a revised draft multiple times can help you make sure you're catching any errors. Use the checklist below to edit your sentences.

✔ Editing Checklist

- ☐ Do all sentences begin with a capital letter and end with a punctuation mark?
- ☐ Are there any comma splices, run-on sentences, or sentence fragments?
- ☐ Are quotation marks used correctly?
- ☐ Are proper nouns capitalized?
- ☐ Did I use transition words and phrases correctly?
- ☐ Are all words spelled correctly?

List two mistakes you found as you proofread your opinion essay.

1 _____

_____

2 _____

_____

Grammar Connections

When you join two independent clauses using only a comma you create a comma splice. You can rewrite the sentence as two simple sentences. How would you fix this sentence? *Social media is good, it helps people keep in touch.* Write your answer in your writer's notebook.

Publish, Present, and Evaluate

Publishing When you **publish** your writing, you create a clean, neat final copy that is free of mistakes. Adding visuals can make your writing more interesting. Consider including photos or graphs to help make your opinion essay more interesting.

Presentation When you are ready to **present** your work, rehearse your presentation. Use the Presenting Checklist to help you.

Evaluate After you publish your writing, use the rubric below to **evaluate** your writing.

What did you do successfully? _____

What needs more work? _____

_____

Presenting Checklist

☐ Stand up straight.

☐ Make eye contact with the audience. Do not stare at your paper.

☐ Pronounce all words clearly.

☐ Speak at a rate that is not too fast.

☐ Speak in a loud enough volume so that everyone can hear you.

4	3	2	1
• clearly introduces a point of view about the topic • presents relevant evidence in logical order to support the claim • addresses an opposing viewpoint and refutes it with sufficient facts	• introduces a point of view about the topic • presents relevant evidence in a mostly logical order to support the claim • addresses an opposing viewpoint and refutes it with a few facts	• does not clearly introduce a point of view about the topic • presents relevant evidence, but not in logical order • addresses an opposing viewpoint but does not use facts to refute it	• does not introduce a point of view about the topic • presents evidence that is not relevant to the claim • does not include an opposing viewpoint

Spiral Review

You have learned new skills and strategies in Unit 1 that will help you read more critically. Now it is time to practice what you have learned.

- **Context Clues**
- **Primary and Secondary Sources**
- **Headings**
- **Cause and Effect**
- **Plot**
- **Make Inferences**

Connect to Content

- **Make a Map**
- **"Take It from Nature"**

Read the selection and choose the best answer to each question.

A Protector of NATURE

[1]   Many people have worked throughout the years to protect our country's natural lands. One such person was Margaret "Mardy" Thomas Murie. Murie was born in Seattle, Washington, on August 18, 1902. Soon after, her family moved to Alaska. First, they moved to Juneau and then later to Fairbanks. Murie's childhood in Alaska was an adventure. The family kept their cabin warm with wood stoves. In the winter, they hung laundry to dry indoors. Those early years in Alaska gave Murie a love of nature that continued throughout her life.

A Woman of Alaska

[2]   When Murie was 18, she left home to go to college in Oregon. But she was never gone for long. She spent her summers in Alaska. Later, she decided to finish college in Alaska. In 1921, she met Olaus Murie. He was a scientist who was studying caribou, a kind of deer. The study was for the U.S. Biological Survey. This is a government group that studies nature. The two wrote letters and planned visits over the next three years. In 1924, Murie became the first woman to graduate from what is now called the University of Alaska. Afterwards, she and Olaus married.

[3]   The marriage between the couple was a working partnership. They spent their three-month honeymoon collecting nature samples in Alaska. Later, Olaus studied grizzly bears while Murie was getting ready to have their first child. Murie laughed when she remembered raising her three children in camping tents: "I didn't have to wax the floor. . . [or] answer the telephone."

New Home in Wyoming

[4]   In 1927, Olaus was asked to study elk, another kind of deer, in Jackson, Wyoming. Murie helped in the camps, assisted Olaus's work, and raised the children. By 1945, Wyoming had become home. The couple bought a ranch in Moose, Wyoming. The ranch sat next to what became the Grand Teton National Park. The ranch was the headquarters of The Wilderness Society. The Muries both helped to direct the Society at different times. The Wilderness Society worked with the government to save natural lands in Alaska. The Muries continued to work with the Society. Their efforts helped lead to the establishment of the Arctic National Wildlife Refuge. The couple also worked to pass the Wilderness Act. This act set up a government process to save natural areas.

A Grandmother Protecting Nature

[5]   In 1963, Olaus died. Murie wanted to honor her late husband by continuing his work. She was there in 1964 when President Lyndon B. Johnson signed the Wilderness Act. Murie went on to become an author, speaker, and public supporter on issues related to protecting natural areas. She sold the Wyoming ranch in 1968. The ranch became part of the Grand Teton National Park. Murie stayed on to found and teach in the Teton Science School. In 1975, she wrote a report that recommended the protection of Alaskan lands.

In 1980, Congress protected millions of acres in Alaska with the Alaska National Interest Lands Conservation Act. Murie said, "Beauty is a resource in and of itself."

[6]   Murie received many awards and honors for her work to protect natural areas. She won the Presidential Medal of Freedom in 1998. This is the highest award that a person not in the military can receive in the United States. Murie died in Wyoming in 2003 at age 101. She is now known to many as the "grandmother" of the movement to protect nature.

Sunny Awazuhara-Reed/Design Pics/age fotostock

1 The word <u>graduate</u> in paragraph 2 means —

   A to finish school

   B to attend school

   C to find a job

   D to become a teacher

2 Read this sentence from paragraph 5.

> *"Beauty is a resource in and of itself."*

The author included this primary source to show the reader —

   F the author's point of view about Murie

   G Murie's point of view in her own words

   H Murie's retelling of another source

   J what other authors have written about Murie

3 What do the subheadings in the article help the reader understand?

   A Murie and her family did not travel much.

   B Alaska was more important to Murie than Wyoming.

   C The author is knowledgeable about the states.

   D All natural places were important to Murie.

> **Quick Tip**
>
> Think about the subheadings in the selection. Then reread paragraphs 4 and 5. Which answer choice does the text best support?

4 What was the effect of the Wilderness Act?

   F Murie became director of the Wilderness Society.

   G Murie sold her Wyoming ranch.

   H The government set up a process to save natural areas.

   J Many people moved away from cities.

Read the selection and choose the best answer to each question.

Solutions, Not
COMPLAINTS

[1]   Sofia woke early. She and her mom were always the first ones in the family to start the morning. The family lived on the outskirts of the city, but Sofia went to school in the center of the city. She needed extra time in the mornings because she had to change from one city bus to another halfway through the ride. She rolled her wheelchair quietly toward the kitchen in search of breakfast. A loud sigh escaped her lips as she rolled up to the table where her mom had prepared a hot breakfast.

[2]   "So much wrong so early in the morning?" Sofia's mother questioned as she started to make a pot of coffee.

[3]   "No, I guess not. I mean, it would just be so much easier to get to school if the light rail train stopped in our neighborhood. We'd get more sleep, anyway," Sofia defended.

[4]   "Maybe that's something you should take up with the mayor," Sofia's mother suggested. She always encouraged solutions over complaints.

[5]   Throughout the school day, Sofia thought about her mother's suggestion. After school during the ride home, Sofia and her mother changed buses for the second time that day. This convinced Sofia that her mother was right. When Sofia arrived home, she gathered a pen and paper to write the mayor.

Dear Mr. Mayor,

6   My name is Sofia Martinez. Every day, I take two buses to and from school. That's right, two. I have to change buses halfway through my trip because there is no direct route. This means that my mom and I miss out on sleep and time with my family in the mornings because we have to leave the house so early. Also, I know that I'm not the only person in my neighborhood who faces this problem. My neighbor works as a nurse at the city hospital. He takes two buses to and from work every day, too.

7   My mom suggested that I write you because I have a solution to this problem. The light rail train route should be extended to include a stop in my neighborhood.

8   I know that this solution will cost money. But I think the cost is worth it. For one thing, it will lower the traffic and pollution in the city. Some people drive cars because they don't want the hassle of changing buses. If they could take the train directly to work, they might leave their cars at home. Also, the train is simple for all kinds of people to use. It is easy to get on and to get off, and the cost to ride is low.

9   Thank you for taking the time to read my letter. Please think about my idea.

Sincerely,

Sofia Martinez

1 How does what Sofia says in paragraph 3 affect the plot?

   A It shows that Sofia is always voicing complaints to her mother.

   B It causes Sofia's mother to recommend a solution that Sofia follows.

   C It explains why Sofia enjoys riding the bus to school every day.

   D It highlights the troubled relationship between Sofia and her mother.

Quick Tip

If you can't decide between two answers, reread the text. Look for evidence that will help you answer the question.

2 The turning point of the story is when —

   F Sofia wakes early in the morning

   G Sofia and her mother discuss their bus trips

   H Sofia decides to write a letter to the mayor

   J Sofia enters the kitchen to eat breakfast

3 What is the solution in Sofia's letter?

   A The light rail train route should be extended.

   B The bus should provide a direct route to school.

   C The bus route should be extended.

   D The light rail train is too expensive to expand.

4 By the end of the story, the reader can infer that —

   F Sofia will not mail her letter to the mayor

   G Sofia's mother is friends with the mayor

   H Sofia's friends live in the city

   J Sofia cares about other people

EXTEND YOUR LEARNING

UNDERSTAND POINT OF VIEW

COLLABORATE

- In the **Literature Anthology**, reread pages 33–34 of *One Hen*.

- When an author writes a story, she or he chooses first- or third-person point of view. A **first-person narrator** is a character in the story and uses pronouns such as *I, me,* and *we.* **A third-person narrator** is a voice outside the story and uses pronouns such as *he, she,* and *they.*

- How would *One Hen* be different if it were told from the first-person point of view? _____

_____

_____

USE NEW VOCABULARY

When you read, you learn new words. Using newly acquired vocabulary in your discussions or writing will help you better understand what they mean.

- Review the vocabulary you learned in Unit 1.
- In your writer's notebook, continue the story "A Fresh Idea." Use at least five vocabulary words you learned in Unit 1 in your response.
- List the vocabulary words you plan to use below.

_____

_____ _____

_____

_____

ANALYZE PLOT

All stories have a beginning, middle, and end. The plot is the sequence of events that make up the story. When you analyze plot elements, you discuss the rising action, climax, falling action, and resolution.

During the **rising action**, the conflict, or problem, begins to build up toward the climax. The **climax** is the turning point or high point of interest in the story. The **falling action** follows the climax and shows the events that lead to the resolution. In the **resolution**, the conflict is resolved, and the story ends.

Analyze the plot elements in *One Hen*. Then complete the chart below.

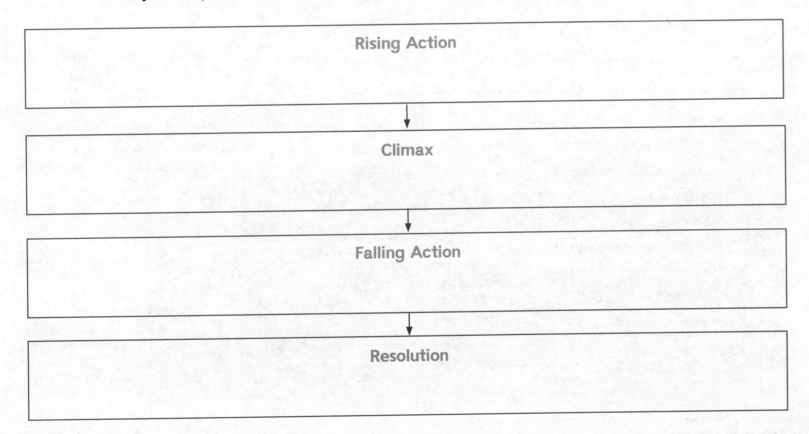

Rising Action

↓

Climax

↓

Falling Action

↓

Resolution

MAKE A MAP

COLLABORATE

Make a map of your school. What directions would you give to a parent to help them arrive at a location in your school, such as the auditorium?

- Tell a partner the steps a person should take after arriving at school.
- Have your partner restate, or repeat, the instructions to you to show that the directions are understood.
- Ask your partner to follow the steps by drawing the path on your map.
- Choose a new location. Your partner will tell you the steps you will restate and record on the map.

What would you include in the key of your map?

_____

_____

_____

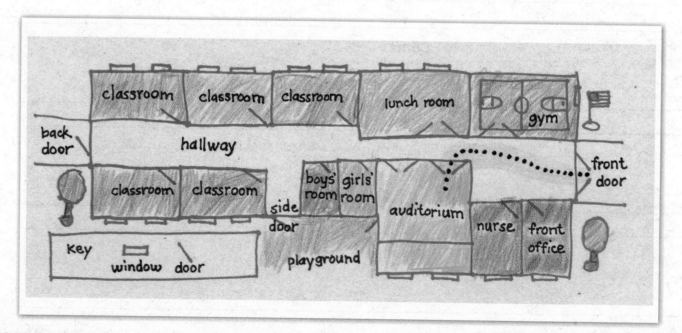

TAKE IT FROM NATURE

COLLABORATE

SOCIAL STUDIES

Digital texts often have elements such as links to other sites or articles. Log on to **my.mheducation.com** and reread the online *Time for Kids* article "Take It from Nature," including the information found in the interactive elements. Answer the questions below.

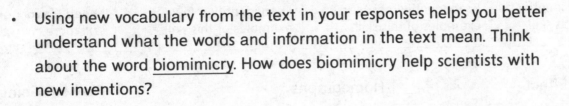

Take It From Nature
Need a problem solved? Ask Mother Nature.

Time for Kids: "Take It from Nature"

- Using new vocabulary from the text in your responses helps you better understand what the words and information in the text mean. Think about the word <u>biomimicry</u>. How does biomimicry help scientists with new inventions?

_____

_____

- Why did engineers in Germany design a new car based on the boxfish?

_____

_____

- Why did engineers in Zimbabwe model new buildings based on termite mounds?

_____

_____

- How can you find information about how the skin of Great White Sharks helped Olympian swimmers?

_____

_____

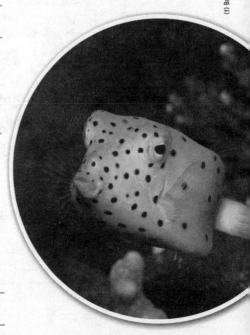

TRACK YOUR PROGRESS

WHAT DID YOU LEARN?

Use the rubric to evaluate yourself on the skills you learned in this unit.
Write your scores in the boxes below.

4	3	2	1
I can successfully identify all examples of this skill.	I can identify most examples of this skill.	I can identify a few examples of this skill.	I need to work on this skill more.

☐ Cause and Effect   ☐ Homographs   ☐ Author's Point of View

☐ Sequence   ☐ Context Clues   ☐ Greek and Latin Prefixes

Something that I need to work more on is _____ because

_____

_____

Text to Self Think back over the texts that you have read in this unit.
Choose one text and write a short paragraph explaining a personal
connection that you have made to the text. Making a personal connection
will deepen your understanding of the text.

I made a personal connection to _____ because _____

_____

_____

SOCIAL STUDIES

Present Your Work

COLLABORATE

Discuss with your group how you will present your debate about the effects of a specific technology. Use the Listening Checklist as your classmates give their presentations. Discuss the sentence starters below and write your answers.

Listening Checklist

☐ Listen carefully to the moderator and follow stated rules.

☐ Listen attentively so you can interpret the message of each speaker.

☐ Listen and respond with respect.

☐ Pay attention to non-verbal messages, such as hand gestures or facial expressions.

☐ Avoid emotional comments unrelated to the topic.

An interesting fact I learned about a specific technology is _____
_____
_____

I would like to know more about _____
_____
_____

asiseeit/E+/Getty Images

Talk About It

Historians do not have a complete record of the past, but it is possible that General George Washington met with Betsy Ross, a seamstress living in Philadelphia during the time of the American Revolution. They, and others, worked together on a proposal for a flag to represent the new nation.

Look at the illustration. Talk with a partner about what Washington, Ross, and the others are doing to solve a problem. Write your ideas in the web.

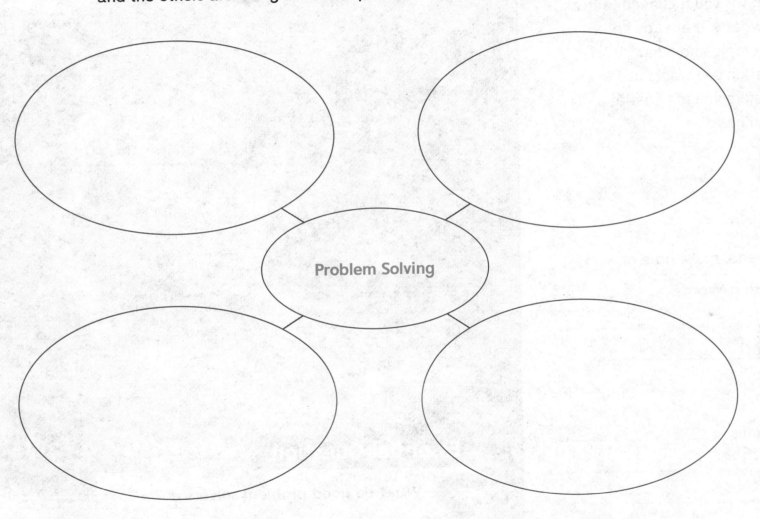

Problem Solving

Go online to **my.mheducation.com** and read the "Meet Me in the Middle" Blast. Think about how you feel when you have to compromise. Why is learning to compromise important? Then blast back your response.

Francis G. Mayer/Corbis/VCG/Getty Images

TAKE NOTES

Asking questions helps you figure out your purpose for reading. It also gives you a chance to think about what you already know about a topic and what information you would like to gain. Before you read, write a question here.

_____

_____

_____

As you read, make note of:

Interesting Words _____

_____

_____

_____

Key Details _____

_____

_____

_____

_____

Creating a Nation

(bkgd) Oleksiy Maksymenko/Alamy; (c) Peter Newark American Pictures/Bridgeman Art Library

Essential Question

?

What do good problem solvers do?

Read about how American colonists tried to solve their problems with Great Britain.

Taxes and Protests

In 1765, King George III of Great Britain needed money to rule his empire. How could he raise it? With taxes! Parliament, the law-making branch of the British government, passed a new tax called the Stamp Act. Every piece of paper sold in the American colonies had to carry a special stamp. Want to buy a newspaper? Stamp! Pay the tax.

To most colonists, the Stamp Act was unfair. The citizens of Great Britain had the right to choose **representatives** to speak for them in Parliament. Although British citizens, the colonists had no such right. How could Parliament tax them if they had no voice in government?

The colonists held protests against the Stamp Act. Consequently, it was repealed, or canceled. But more taxes followed. Women protested a tax on cloth imported from Britain. How? They wove their own cloth at home.

Boston Tea Party: Colonists throw tea into the harbor.

Before long, the **situation** grew worse. In 1770, British soldiers fired into a disorderly crowd in Boston. Five colonists died. This tragedy is known as the Boston Massacre.

By 1773, most taxes had been repealed, or canceled, except the one on tea. One night, colonists held a protest called the Boston Tea Party. Dressed in disguise, they slipped onto three British ships in Boston Harbor and then they tossed the ships' cargo—tea—overboard.

Anonymous/Getty Images

FIND TEXT EVIDENCE

Read

Paragraphs 1-2

Problem and Solution

Underline the problem King George III faced. Write it here.

_____

_____

Circle the king's solution to the problem. Discuss why the colonists thought the Stamp Act was unfair.

_____

_____

_____

Paragraphs 3-5

Reread

Draw a box around text evidence that tells how the colonists reacted to taxes imposed by the British.

Reread

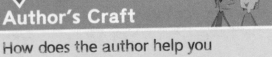

Author's Craft

How does the author help you understand the relationship between the British and the colonists?

FIND TEXT EVIDENCE

Read

Paragraphs 1-2

Problem and Solution

Circle the ways in which colonists differed on how to solve and resolve problems with the king. Based on this information, what inference can you make about the mood in the colonies at that time?

_____

_____

_____

Paragraphs 3-5

Reread

Underline the names of the two people appointed by Congress to help with the conflict.

Reread

Author's Craft

Why is "Revolution Begins" a good heading for this section?

Revolution Begins

An angry King George punished the colonies by ordering the port of Boston closed and town meetings banned. Colonists called these harsh actions the "Intolerable Acts." However, they could not agree on how to **resolve** the problems with Great Britain. Patriots wanted to fight for independence. Loyalists wanted peace with the king. Many colonists were undecided.

Finally, colonists called for representatives from each colony to attend a **convention**. This important meeting, the First Continental Congress, took place in 1774 in Philadelphia. After discussion, the delegates decided to send a peace **proposal** to the king. Congress ended, but the trouble continued. In April 1775, there were rumors that the British were marching to Lexington and Concord, villages near Boston, to capture weapons that the patriots had hidden there.

The colonial militias were ready. Militias were groups of volunteers willing to fight. British troops attacked. The militias fired back. Surprisingly, the British retreated, or went back.

Now that war had begun, the patriots called for a Second Continental Congress in May. Delegates made George Washington commander of the new Continental Army. Congress also sent another peace proposal to King George.

As war continued, Congress formed **committees** to do important tasks. Five delegates were chosen to write a declaration of independence. This committee gave the job to one of its members—Thomas Jefferson.

Oleksiy Maksymenko/Alamy

Events of the American Revolution

1765	1766	1770	1773	1774	1775	1776	1778
Passage of Stamp Act	Repeal of Stamp Act	Boston Massacre	Boston Tea Party / The First Continental Congress		• The Battle of Lexington and Concord / • Start of the Second Continental Congress	Declaration of Independence	Alliance with France

Independence Declared

Jefferson knew he had to convince many colonists of the need for independence. As a result, he combined a variety of ideas to make his case. Individuals, he explained, had certain rights. These included life, liberty, and the pursuit of happiness. Governments were created to protect those rights. Instead, King George had taken away colonists' rights and freedoms. Therefore, the colonies had to separate from Britain.

Congress went on to **debate** Jefferson's points. As a result, his strong words against slavery were deleted. There were other compromises, too. But on July 4, 1776, Congress approved the Declaration of Independence. A nation was born. Washington's army fought on. Finally, in 1778, France joined the fight on America's side.

This was a turning point. In 1781, British troops surrendered in the war's last major battle. That year, Congress approved the Articles of Confederation. This document outlined a government for the former colonies. The United States was created as a confederation, or a **union**, of separate states. The Articles gave the states, rather than a central government, the power to make most decisions.

In 1783, King George finally recognized the nation's independence. By then, though, the United States government clearly wasn't working very well. The states often didn't agree with one another.

The revolution had ended. The work of shaping a government had just started. It would continue with a Constitutional Convention in 1787.

Timeline

1781
- Last major battle of the war
- Approval of the Articles of Confederation

1783
- King George recognizes independence of United States

Summarize

Use your notes and the timeline to orally summarize the important events in "Creating a Nation."

FIND TEXT EVIDENCE 🔍

Read
Paragraphs 1–5
Context Clues

Circle context clues that help you determine the meaning of *liberty*.

Timeline

Look at the timeline. Did the Boston Tea Party take place before the repeal of the Stamp Act or after?

Reread

Author's Craft

How does the author help you understand that things were changing for the colonists?

Fluency

Read aloud the first paragraph on page 103 to a partner. Discuss what helps you read the paragraph fluently with accuracy.

Vocabulary

Use the example sentences to talk with a partner about each word. Then answer the questions.

committees

I am on one of the **committees** to plan our winter class trip.

What committees could help to plan a school talent show?

_____

_____

convention

We learned the difference between bugs and insects at the science **convention**.

What are two words that mean the same as convention?

_____

_____

debate

My classmates like to **debate**, or discuss their different opinions.

What words help you know what debate means?

_____

_____

proposal

The mayor shared a new **proposal** to build a library.

What proposal can you make to raise money for the field trip?

_____

_____

representatives

Our government **representatives** help to make and pass laws.

Who is the fifth grade representative on the student council?

_____

_____

 Build Your Word List Reread the first paragraph on page 102. Circle the word _Patriots_. In your writer's notebook, use a word web to write more forms of the word. For example, write _patriotic_. Use a dictionary to help you find more related words.

resolve

To **resolve** the argument over our food choices, Ms. Smith asked Joe to look up facts on nutrition.

Who helps you to resolve a problem?

_____

_____

situation

The icy roads caused a dangerous driving **situation**.

What kind of weather can cause a serious flooding situation?

_____

_____

union

The United States is a **union** of 50 states that joined together.

What two U.S. states are not physically joined to the rest of the union?

_____

_____

Context Clues

Writers may define or restate the meaning of a difficult word by using commas and the clue word *or*. At other times, they may define the word in a nearby sentence.

FIND TEXT EVIDENCE

I'm not sure what repealed *means in the sentence* "By 1773 most taxes had been repealed, or canceled, except the one on tea." *But I see from the comma and the words* or canceled *that* repealed *means "canceled."*

By 1773 most taxes had been repealed, or canceled, except the one on tea.

Your Turn Use context clues to figure out the meanings of the following words in "Creating a Nation."

Parliament, page 101 _____

_____

retreated, page 102 _____

_____

Reread

As you read, you should monitor your comprehension to make sure you understand the meaning of the text. When you read something that confuses you, you may have to go back and reread an earlier part of the selection. Rereading can help you check your understanding of facts and details in "Creating a Nation."

Quick Tip

The topic sentence in each paragraph can be used to help you monitor your comprehension. As you read, pay attention to how the details in the rest of the paragraph relate to the topic sentence.

🔍 FIND TEXT EVIDENCE

When you read the second paragraph of the section "Revolution Begins" on page 102, you may be confused about why the British troops began marching to Lexington and Concord.

Page 102

After discussion, the delegates decided to send a peace **proposal** to the king. Congress ended, but the trouble continued.

When I reread <u>the delegates decided to send a peace proposal to the king. Congress ended, but the trouble continued</u>, *I ask myself, "Why did the trouble continue even though the delegates sent a peace plan?" I can make the inference that King George did not agree to the proposal.*

Your Turn Reread page 102. Discuss and retell how the patriots responded to the British troops marching to Lexington and Concord. What happened after the British troops attacked? Reread to find the answer.

_____

_____

_____

Headings and Timelines

The selection "Creating a Nation" is expository text. Expository text gives facts, examples, and explanations about a topic. It may include text features such as headings, charts, diagrams, or timelines that organize information.

Readers to Writers

Writers use headings and timelines to give readers a quick overview of information. How can you use these text features in your own writing?

🔍 FIND TEXT EVIDENCE

I can tell that "Creating a Nation" is expository text because it gives facts about events that led up to and followed the American Revolution. I also see headings and a timeline.

Page 102

Revolution Begins

An angry King George punished the colonies by ordering the port of Boston closed and town meetings banned. Colonists called these harsh actions the "Intolerable Acts." However, they could not agree on how to **resolve** the problems with Great Britain. Patriots wanted to fight for independence. Loyalists wanted peace with the king. Many colonists were undecided.

Finally, colonists called for representatives from each colony to attend a **convention**. This important meeting, the First Continental Congress, took place in 1774 in Philadelphia. After discussion, the delegates decided to send a peace **proposal** to the king. Congress ended, but the trouble continued. In April 1775, there were rumors that the British were marching to Lexington and Concord, villages near Boston, to capture weapons that the patriots had hidden there.

The colonial militias were ready. Militias were groups of volunteers willing to fight. British troops attacked. The militias fired back. Surprisingly, the British retreated, or went back.

Now that war had begun, the patriots called for a Second Continental Congress in May. Delegates made George Washington commander of the new Continental Army. Congress also sent another peace proposal to King George.

As war continued, Congress formed **committees** to do important tasks. Five delegates were chosen to write a declaration of independence. This committee gave the job to one of its members—Thomas Jefferson.

Events of the American Revolution

| 1765 | 1766 | 1770 | 1773 | 1774 | 1775 | 1776 | 1778 |

Passage of Stamp Act

Repeal of Stamp Act

Boston Massacre

Boston Tea Party

The First Continental Congress

• The Battle of Lexington and Concord
• Start of the Second Continental Congress

Declaration of Independence

Alliance with France

Headings

A heading tells what a section of text is mostly about.

Timeline

A timeline is a diagram that shows events in the order they took place.

Your Turn Review and discuss the events on the timeline. Why did the author include the timeline? How is the information helpful?

Problem and Solution

When an author uses a **problem** and **solution** text structure, the author presents a problem and then tells the solution, or the steps taken to solve the problem. Signal words and phrases, such as *consequently, as a result, therefore,* and *so,* can help you identify the solution.

🔍 FIND TEXT EVIDENCE

When I read "Independence Declared" on page 103, I realize that Thomas Jefferson's problem was to convince undecided colonists of the need for independence. The signal words as a result *tell me that I will read Jefferson's solution:* He combined a variety of ideas to make his case for independence.

Problem	Solution
Some colonists didn't want independence.	Jefferson combined ideas to convince them.

Your Turn Reread "Creating a Nation." Find other problems faced by the colonists and list them in your graphic organizer on page 109. Then identify how the colonists solved the problems.

Peter Newark American Pictures/Bridgeman Art Library

Problem	Solution

Respond to Reading

COLLABORATE

Discuss the prompt below. Think about how the author presents the information. Use your notes and graphic organizer to write a response that is a paragraph long.

How does the author help you see how the relationship between the British and the colonists changed?

_____

_____

_____

_____

_____

_____

_____

_____

_____

_____

_____

_____

_____

_____

Use these sentence starters to discuss the text and to put your text evidence in order.

- *At first, the colonists . . .*
- *Then I read that . . .*
- *Finally, the colonists . . .*

Grammar Connections

As you write your response, be sure to check that you have capitalized the names of people and the initials that stand for their names.

John Quincy Adams

J.Q. Adams

Remember that titles or abbreviations of titles, when they come before or after the names of people, are capitalized.

Mr. Jefferson

King George III

Primary and Secondary Sources

Primary sources help us learn about the past. A primary source may be an original document or an account by someone who took part in an event. Here are some examples of primary sources:

*   photographs and maps from the time being studied
*   letters and diary entries
*   autobiographies

What is another example of a primary source? Write your answer.

_____

_____

The image above shows a part of the Declaration of Independence. Which part of the document is shown? Write your answer below.

_____

_____

_____

Secondary sources are created by someone who does not have firsthand knowledge of the topic. Secondary sources include textbooks and encyclopedias.

Make a Poster With a partner or in a group, make a poster or multimodal slideshow, one that includes words, pictures, and sounds, about the creation of the U.S. Constitution. Include important facts about the Constitution, such as the answers to these questions.

*   What is the U.S. Constitution?
*   Who drafted it?
*   Why was it written?
*   Where and when were the meetings held?

Discuss what primary and secondary sources you might use in your research and why. Add photos, illustrations, and music to your poster or slideshow. After you finish, you will be sharing your work with the class.

_____

_____

National Archives and Records Administration

Who Wrote the U.S. Constitution?

? How does the sidebar give you more insight into the role James
Madison played in the Virginia Plan?

*Literature Anthology:
pages 96–111*

COLLABORATE

Talk About It Reread **Literature Anthology** page 103. Discuss what the
information in the sidebar tells you.

Cite Text Evidence Which words and phrases in the sidebar tell you more
about James Madison? Write text evidence and tell why it's important.

Text Evidence	Why It's Important

Make Inferences

Sidebars provide
information that helps you
to better understand the
main text. What inference
can you make about James
Madison based on the
information in the sidebar
and the main text?

Write The author uses the sidebar to _____

_____

_____

How does the author build suspense in "The Great Compromise"?

Talk About It Reread **Literature Anthology** page 104. Discuss how the author describes what happened on July 2, 1787.

Cite Text Evidence Which words and phrases does the author use to create suspense? Write text evidence in the chart.

Text Evidence	How It Builds Suspense

Write The author builds suspense by _____

_____

_____

Quick Tip

Think about the events of July 2, 1787. Why are the states tied? How does this create suspense?

 Synthesize Information

Combine what you already know about language with what you find in the text to create a new understanding. Think about what words signal suspense. Consider why the author chose to use those words in a social studies text.

? **How does the author use an anecdote to help you understand how Benjamin Franklin's outlook changes?**

Talk About It Reread the last two paragraphs on page 110 of the **Literature Anthology**. Discuss what Franklin thought about the carving on Washington's chair.

Cite Text Evidence How does what Franklin thinks about the carving indicate that his outlook changed? Use text evidence to explain.

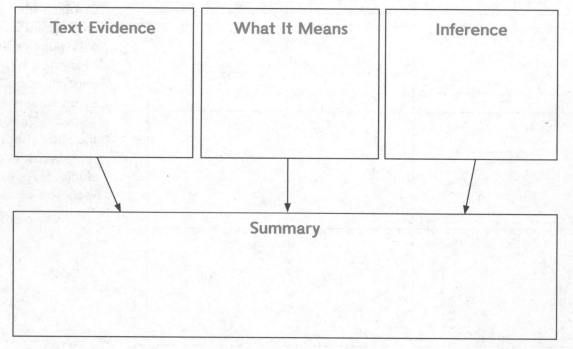

Text Evidence	What It Means	Inference

Summary

Write The anecdote helps me understand how Benjamin Franklin's outlook has changed by showing _____

_____

_____

Respond to Reading

COLLABORATE

Discuss the prompt below. Apply your own knowledge of compromise to inform your answer. Use your notes and graphic organizer.

How does the author help you understand that the decisions the delegates made affected not only them but all Americans?

_____

_____

_____

_____

_____

_____

_____

_____

_____

_____

_____

_____

_____

_____

Yulia Reznikov/Alamy

Quick Tip

Use these sentence starters to talk about and cite text evidence.

- *Candice Ransom uses text features to . . .*
- *She creates suspense by . . .*
- *This helps me see that the delegates . . .*

Self-Selected Reading

Choose a text and fill in your writer's notebook with the title, author, and genre. Include a personal response to the text in your writer's notebook. A personal response might include an experience you had that is similar to what you read. It might also include how you feel about what you are reading.

Wordsmiths

Literature Anthology: pages 114–117

1   Terry regularly used her voice to resolve problems and fight for social equality. When white neighbors attempted to claim the Princes' land as their own, they took their neighbors to court to address the situation. "Bars Fight," her only surviving poem, established Terry as the first African American female poet in the United States. Remembered as a woman who brought words to life, Terry died in 1821 in Sunderland, Vermont.

2   Terry's remarkable life was celebrated in *The Franklin Herald* of Greenfield, Massachusetts, with a lengthy obituary. The following excerpt was reprinted in *The Vermont Gazette*.

3   *In this remarkable woman there was an assemblage of qualities rarely to be found... Her volubility [ability to speak continuously] was exceeded by none, and in general the fluency of her speech was not destitute [lacking] of instruction and education. She was much respected among her acquaintance, who treated her with a degree of deference.*

Reread paragraph 1. **Underline** words and phrases that describe Lucy Terry Prince.

Reread paragraph 2. **Circle** the word that shows the author admires Terry.

Reread paragraph 3. **Draw a box** around the sentence that tells how people felt about the poet. Write the sentence here:

_____

_____

_____

COLLABORATE

Talk with a partner about Lucy Terry Prince's accomplishments. Discuss and retell the qualities of Lucy Terry Prince. Write them here:

_____

_____

_____

bayram/Getty Images

1 Wheatley is remembered as the first African American to publish a collection of poetry. She also wrote and sent a poem to General George Washington in 1775 that praised him for his success during the American Revolution. His response to her shows how highly regarded Wheatley was. Below is part of Washington's letter.

2 Mrs Phillis,

I thank you most sincerely for your polite notice of me, in the elegant Lines you enclosed; and however undeserving I may be...

3 If you should ever come to Cambridge, or near Head Quarters, I shall be happy to see a person so favoured [well liked] by the Muses [inspirational forces]...

–G. Washington

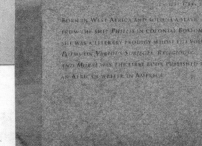

Statue of Phillis Wheatley

Reread paragraph 1. **Circle** the reason why Wheatley is remembered. Write it here:

_____

_____

_____

Reread paragraph 2. **Underline** George Washington's description of Wheatley's poem.

COLLABORATE

Talk with a partner about George Washington's letter to Wheatley. Did he indicate that he enjoyed her poem? How do you know? Write your answer here:

_____

_____

_____

_____

_____

? **What is the author's purpose for writing about the two poets?**

COLLABORATE

Talk About It Reread the excerpts on pages 116 and 117. Talk with a partner about the accomplishments of the two poets.

Cite Text Evidence What words and phrases does the author use to describe each poet? Write text evidence in the chart.

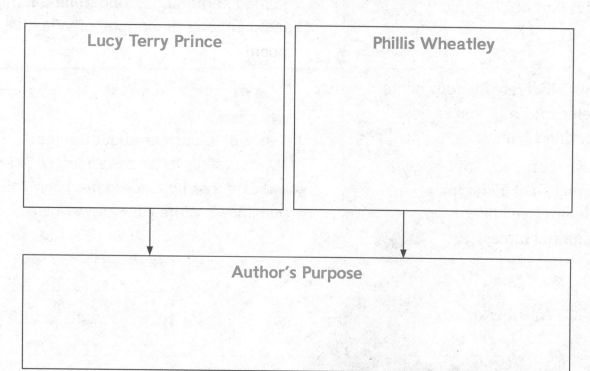

Lucy Terry Prince	Phillis Wheatley

Author's Purpose

Write The author's purpose for writing about these two poets is _____

_____

_____

Samuel Borges Photography/Shutterstock.com

Print and Graphic Features

Writers include **print** and **graphic** features to make their pieces more interesting and to support the information. Some features include primary sources, such as obituaries and letters from the time period. Photographs also can help writers tell their story.

FIND TEXT EVIDENCE

On page 116, paragraph 3 contains an excerpt from Lucy Terry Prince's obituary. The author includes this piece because it gives evidence of the respect Terry earned during her lifetime.

> *In this remarkable woman there was an assemblage of qualities rarely to be found...*

Your Turn Reread paragraph 2 on page 117. Look at the photograph of the sculpture.

COLLABORATE

- How does George Washington's letter strengthen the idea that Phillis Wheatley was a notable poet? _____

_____

_____

- How does the sculpture of Phillis Wheatley support the author's point of view about her? _____

_____

Text Connections

? **What have you learned about how people solve problems?**

Quick Tip

Talk about how problems get solved. Use clues in the photograph and ideas you read about to help you.

Talk About It Think about the selections you read. Look at the photograph and read the caption. Talk with a partner about the problems with keeping the Liberty Bell safe.

Cite Text Evidence With a partner, **draw arrows** pointing at two things that protect the Liberty Bell. **Circle** text evidence in the caption that tells one way.

Write The selections I read and this photograph help me understand how people solve problems by _____

_____

_____

_____

_____

_____

Visitors must pass through a security checkpoint before they walk past the Liberty Bell at the Liberty Bell Center in Philadelphia, PA.

NPS Photo

SOCIAL STUDIES

Present Your Work

COLLABORATE

Discuss how you will present your poster or multimodal slideshow about the Constitution. Show that you understand the credibility of the primary and secondary source materials by pointing out which you found the most reliable. Use the Presenting Checklist as you practice your presentation. Discuss the sentence starters below and write your answers.

Quick Tip

Plan your rehearsal so that you allow time for questions and feedback. Practice will improve your presentation and give you the confidence to do the best you can.

An interesting fact that I learned about the Constitution is _____

_____

_____

I would like to know more about _____

_____

_____

✓ Presenting Checklist

☐ Rehearse your presentation in front of another person. Ask for feedback.

☐ Speak slowly, clearly, and with appropriate tone and expression.

☐ Emphasize points so that the audience can follow important ideas.

☐ Make eye contact with the audience. Do not just look at your poster or slideshow.

☐ Listen carefully to questions from the audience.

☐ Use formal language in your presentation.

Expert Model

Literature Anthology: pages 96–111

Features of an Expository Essay

An expository essay informs readers by presenting a clear central idea and information about a topic. An expository essay

- has an introduction that makes the reader want to keep reading

- presents facts, details, and information in a logical order

- provides a conclusion that relates to the topic

Word Wise

On page 98, author Candice Ransom uses content words such as *borders, governments,* and *taxes.* Using content words and literal language gives her writing a formal tone. Literal language means exactly what it says. For example, *Many people worked together to develop the U.S. Constitution.*

Analyze an Expert Model Studying expository texts will help you learn how to write an expository essay. **Reread** the first paragraph of "A New Plan" on page 98 of *Who Wrote the U.S. Constitution?* in the **Literature Anthology**. Write your answers below.

How does the author use the first two sentences to capture the reader's attention? _____

_____

_____

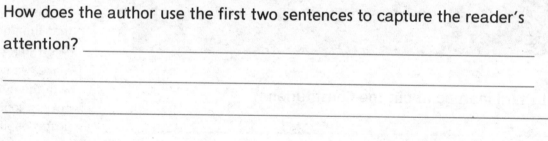

Which detail in the paragraph is the most interesting? Why? _____

_____

_____

_____

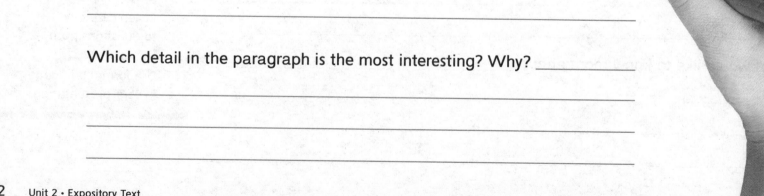

Plan: Choose Your Topic

Brainstorm With a partner, brainstorm a list of people who contributed to the U.S. Constitution. Use your notes on *Who Wrote the U.S. Constitution?* in your discussion. Use these sentence starters to get started.

Some of the most important delegates were . . .

One of the people who . . .

I know this because I read . . .

Writing Prompt Choose one person from your list. Write an essay explaining how that person contributed to the creation of the U.S. Constitution.

I will write about ______________________________.

Purpose and Audience An author's purpose is his or her main reason for writing. Look at the three purposes for writing below. **Underline** your purpose for writing expository text.

to inform, or teach   to persuade, or convince   to entertain

Think about the audience for your essay. Who will read it?

My audience will be ______________________________.

I will use ____________________ language when I write my essay.

Plan In your writer's notebook, make a Main Idea and Detail chart to plan your writing. Fill in the Main Idea box.

Quick Tip

Thinking about your audience will help you decide what tone to use in your writing. Do you use formal language when you text or call a friend? Use literal and formal language when you are writing for a serious purpose such as for reports and letters to your teacher. Use informal language when you are speaking or writing to friends.

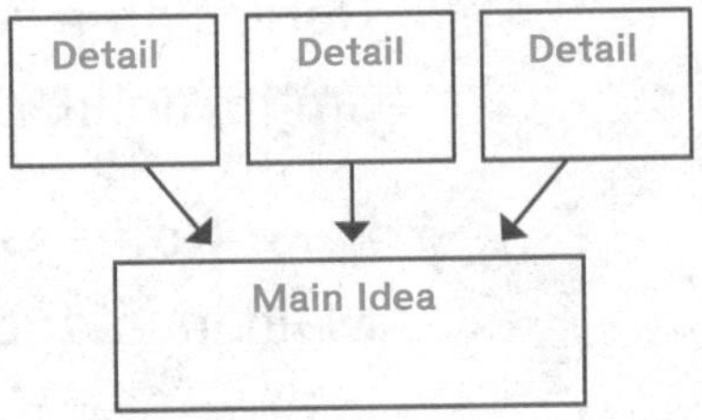

Plan: Research

Choose and Evaluate Sources You will need to research your topic before you begin to write. Make sure you choose reliable sources, such as encyclopedias, websites, and other electronic sources, interviews, books, and periodicals. Compare facts from two reliable sources. If the two sources disagree, find a third source. To check that your sources are reliable, answer these questions:

•   Is the information accurate and current?

•   Does the information give me what I need to know about my topic?

•   Is this material too difficult? Do I need to find another source?

List two sources that you will use.

1 _____

2 _____

Bibliography You will need to develop a bibliography. A bibliography lists all the print and multimedia sources you use for your expository essay. Here is an example bibliography entry for a book:

Smith, John. *Colonial America*. New York: Example Books, 2014.

Take Notes Once you pick your sources, take notes, and fill in your Main Idea and Details chart. When you take notes, paraphrase the information by putting it into your own words. Include only the most important information and keep your notes brief.

Draft

Supporting Details Authors use details to support the central, or main, idea. Supporting details may include facts, definitions, examples, or quotations. In the example below from "Creating a Nation," the author gives details about Thomas Jefferson.

> Jefferson knew he had to convince many colonists of the need for independence. As a result, he combined a variety of ideas to make his case. Individuals, he explained, had certain rights. These included life, liberty, and the pursuit of happiness. Governments were created to protect those rights.

Now use the above paragraph as a model to write about the person you chose for your topic. In the first sentence, give the name of the person you chose. Try to use details to support your central idea in your paragraph.

_____

_____

_____

_____

_____

Write a Draft Use your Main Idea and Details graphic organizer to help you write your draft in your writer's notebook. Don't forget to write a conclusion that restates the central idea and summarizes the details.

Grammar Connections

Use quotation marks (" ") before and after the exact words that a speaker says or writes. Place a period (.), question mark (?), or exclamation mark (!) in the quotation marks when it is part of the quote.

Revise

Quick Tip

Use transition words to help connect your ideas in a clear way. Use transition words and phrases such as *however, therefore, next, as a result,* and *finally.*

Logical Order Effective writers make sure that they present their facts and ideas in a logical order. They provide a conclusion, a paragraph at the end of the text that summarizes the main idea and important details. Read the paragraph below. Then revise it by rearranging ideas and facts so that they are in the most logical order.

> The militias of the colonies were ready. British troops attacked. Militias willing to fight were groups of volunteers. Surprisingly, the British retreated.

 Revision Revise your draft, and check that you present your facts and ideas in a logical order. Check that any dates you give appear in the correct sequence, or order. Remember to use transitions to make your ideas clear and coherent. Don't forget to write a strong, clear conclusion.

Peer Conferences

Review a Draft Listen carefully as a partner reads his or her work aloud. Take notes about what you liked and what was difficult to follow. Begin by telling what you liked about the draft. Ask questions that will help the writer think more about the writing. Make suggestions that you think will make the writing stronger. Use these sentence starters.

I enjoyed this part of your draft because . . .

Some other details you can add are . . .

This part is unclear to me. Can you explain why . . . ?

Partner Feedback After your partner gives you feedback on your draft, write one of the suggestions that you will use in your revision. Refer to the rubric on page 129 as you give feedback.

Based on my partner's feedback, I will _____

_____

After you finish giving each other feedback, reflect on the peer conference. What was helpful? What might you do differently next time?

Revision As you revise your draft use the Revising Checklist to help you figure out what text you may need to move, elaborate on, or delete. Remember to use the rubric on page 129 to help you with your revision.

Revising Checklist

- ☐ Does my writing fit my purpose and audience?
- ☐ What details can I add or delete to make this section clearer?
- ☐ Did I use transitions to show the connections between ideas?
- ☐ Did I rearrange ideas in a clear and coherent way?
- ☐ Did I write a conclusion that sums up my ideas?

Digital Tools

For more information on how to do a peer conference, watch the "Peer Conferencing" video. Go to **my.mheducation.com**.

Edit and Proofread

When you **edit** and **proofread** your writing, you look for and correct mistakes in spelling, punctuation, capitalization, and grammar. Reading through a revised draft multiple times can help you make sure you're catching any errors. Use the checklist below to edit your sentences.

✓ Editing Checklist

- ☐ Do all sentences begin with a capital letter and end with a punctuation mark?
- ☐ Are there any run-on sentences or sentence fragments?
- ☐ Are singular, plural, collective, and irregular nouns used correctly?
- ☐ Are proper nouns capitalized?
- ☐ Are possessive nouns used correctly?
- ☐ Are all words spelled correctly?

List two mistakes you found as you proofread your essay.

1 _____

_____

2 _____

_____

Tech Tip

Spell checkers are useful tools in word-processing programs, but they may not recognize wrong words such as *there* when you mean *they're*. Spell checkers don't replace a careful reading to find errors.

Grammar Connections

When you proofread your essay, make sure that you have capitalized all the proper nouns. Capitalize historic events, periods of time, documents, and nationalities.

Publish, Present, and Evaluate

Publishing When you **publish** your writing, you create a clean, neat final copy that is free of mistakes. Adding visuals can make your writing more interesting. Consider including illustrations, photos, or maps to help make your essay more interesting.

Presentation When you are ready to **present** your work, rehearse your presentation. Use the Presenting Checklist to help you.

Evaluate After you publish your writing, use the rubric below to **evaluate** your writing.

What did you do successfully? _____

What needs more work? _____

_____

4	3	2	1
• gives an informative, interesting, and detailed explanation of a topic using a clear central idea • writing includes facts and details to inform • provides a strong, clear conclusion	• informs readers about a topic using a clear central idea • most of the writing includes facts and details to inform • conclusion is missing a key detail	• makes an effort to inform readers, but the central idea is unclear • very few facts or details to inform • conclusion is not clear	• does not inform readers • no facts or details to inform • does not provide a conclusion

COLLABORATE

Look at the photograph. What task is the man doing? How might he have started his work? How do you think he will complete it?

Talk with a partner about how a plan helps provide guidance for a task. Fill in the web with ideas that describe some things you need to do when planning a successful outcome for a task.

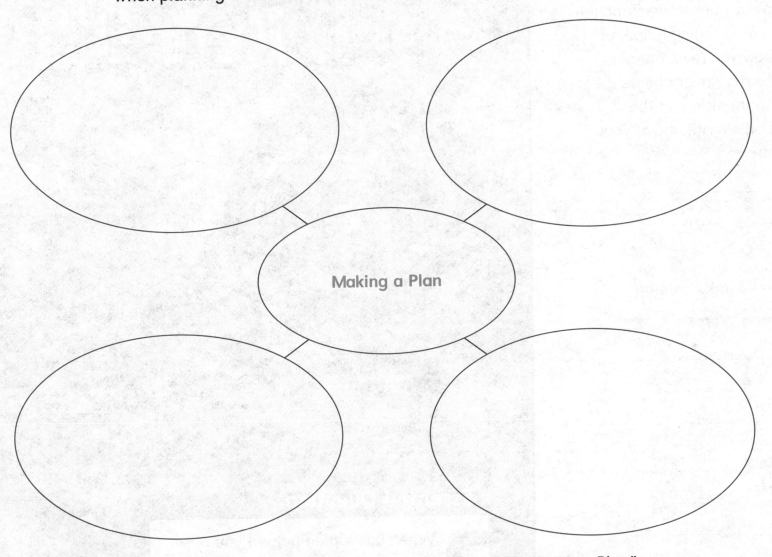

Making a Plan

BLAST
BACK!
studysync

Go online to **my.mheducation.com** and read the "Stand By Your Plan" Blast. Think about how long it took to build the Panama Canal. How do you think having a good plan helps make a huge project a success? Then blast back your response.

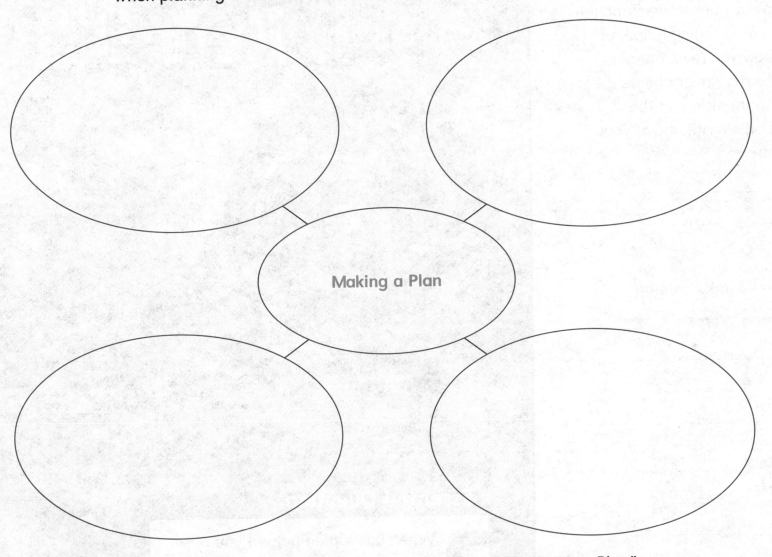
imagebroker.net/SuperStock

TAKE NOTES

Set a purpose for reading before you begin a story. Understanding why you are reading helps you adjust how you read. Imagine what the story might be about based on the title and the illustrations. Write one of your ideas here.

_____

_____

_____

As you read, take note of:

Interesting Words _____

_____

_____

_____

Key Details _____

_____

_____

_____

_____

The Magical Lost Brocade

Essential Question

?

When has a plan helped you accomplish a task?

Read about how Ping follows a plan to find a lost brocade.

Long ago, in China, a poor woman and her son, Ping, lived in a tiny hut. The woman earned a living weaving beautiful brocade hangings, which her son sold. She wished she could give Ping a better home, but alas, that was impossible. So she decided to weave a brocade of a magnificent house with gardens. At least they could look at something lovely. It took three years to complete the brocade, and it was her finest work. However, soon afterward, a great wind swept into their hut and carried it away! The woman was grief-stricken. So Ping went off in **pursuit** of the brocade, **assuring** his mother he would bring it home.

Ping walked for three days and came to a stone house. A bearded man sat outside. "I'm searching for my mother's brocade," Ping said.

"A brocade flew by three days ago," said the man. "Now it's in a palace far away. I'll explain how you can get there and lend you my horse." Ping thanked the man and bowed deeply to express his **gratitude.**

"First, you must ride through Fire Valley," said the man. "You must cross over it regardless of the scorching heat, without uttering a word. If you utter even a single sound, you'll burn!" He continued, "After you've crossed Fire Valley, you'll arrive at Ice Ocean. You must ride through the icy waters without shivering. If you shiver even once, the **outcome** will be terrible! The sea will swallow you up!" The old man paused before concluding, "When you emerge from the sea, you'll be facing the Mountain of the Sun. The mountain is as steep as a straight line up to the sky! The palace sits on top of the mountain, and the brocade is in the palace."

FIND TEXT EVIDENCE

Read

Paragraph 1

Make Predictions

Do you think Ping will find the brocade? Explain your answer.

_____

_____

Paragraphs 2–3

Theme

Underline a sentence that shows Ping trusts the man. What might the author's message be?

_____

_____

Paragraph 4

Setting

Circle the places that tell what kind of story this is.

Reread

Author's Craft

How does the author make Fire Valley and Ice Ocean seem nearly impossible for a person to cross?

FIND TEXT EVIDENCE

Read

Paragraph 1

Theme

Underline the words Ping uses to describe the journey and what he will do. What is the author's message?

_____

_____

Paragraph 2

Personification

Circle the words that make Ice Ocean seem human.

Paragraphs 3–4

Make Inferences

Why do you think Princess Ling did not return the brocade herself?

_____

_____

Reread

Author's Craft

How does the story's mood change when Ping meets Princess Ling?

"It sounds like an extremely difficult journey," said Ping, "but I'll do my very best." He mounted the horse and traveled for three days, reaching the Fire Valley. As he crossed the valley, angry flames leaped out at him. The intense heat brought tears to Ping's eyes, but he said nothing.

When he reached the other side of the valley, he saw the Ice Ocean. With Ping's gentle **guidance,** the horse entered the frigid waters. The sea touched Ping with icy fingers, but he didn't shiver once. So horse and rider crossed the sea, **emerging** safely on the other side.

Next, Ping approached the Mountain of the Sun. He rode up the steep mountain, grasping the reins for dear life! Finally, he reached the top and dismounted at the palace door.

A lovely princess welcomed him. "I'm Princess Ling," she said. "I thought your mother's brocade was beautiful and wanted to copy it. So I sent a great wind to your home. I've now copied the brocade, so please take it home. Have a safe journey."

"Thank you," said Ping, who stared at the beautiful princess. She was a perfect rose. He wondered if he could see her again and **detected** a knowing smile on her face as they said good-bye.

Ping mounted his horse, placing the brocade under his jacket. First, he rode down the steep Mountain of the Sun. Next, he rode back across Ice Ocean, without shivering once. Then he rode across Fire Valley, without making a sound. Finally, he arrived at the home of the bearded man, who sat outside just as he had the **previous** time. Ping thanked him, returned his horse, and began the long walk home.

Ping arrived home three days later. "Here is your brocade, Mother!" he announced as she cried tears of joy. Together, they unrolled it, and before their eyes, the brocade came to life! Suddenly their hut became a magnificent house with gardens. But that wasn't all—standing before them was Princess Ling! Ping and the princess got married, and a year later, Ping's mother became a loving grandmother. They all lived happily together in their beautiful home and gardens!

Summarize

Use your notes to orally summarize the order of events in the story and to describe the main character.

FIND TEXT EVIDENCE

Read

Paragraph 1

Make Predictions

Do you think Ping will see Princess Ling again?

_____

_____

Underline a clue in the first paragraph that you used to make your prediction.

Paragraphs 2–3

Theme

What is the author's message at the end of the story?

_____

_____

Draw a box around the text evidence.

Reread

Author's Craft

Do you think the author's ending was a good one? Why or why not?

Vocabulary

Use the example sentences to talk with a partner about each word. Then answer the questions.

assuring

One job of coaching is **assuring** athletes that they will do well.

What might a coach say when assuring a team?

_____

_____

detected

By the way he sniffed, I knew my dog **detected** another animal.

What have you detected just by hearing?

_____

_____

emerging

I watched as the chick was **emerging** from its shell.

What word or phrase has the same meaning as emerging?

_____

_____

gratitude

I gave flowers to my aunt to show my **gratitude** for her help.

What are other ways people show their gratitude?

_____

_____

guidance

With my Uncle Rico's **guidance**, I learned how to play the guitar.

Whose guidance has helped you learn a new skill?

_____

_____

Build Your Word List Reread the fourth paragraph on page 133. Circle the word *arrive*. In your writer's notebook, use a word web to write more forms of the word. For example, write *arrival*. Use an online or print dictionary to find more words that are related.

outcome

The team was pleased with the **outcome** of the game.

When has the outcome of a game surprised you?

_____

_____

_____

previous

My older brother was the **previous** owner of my bike.

What was the name of your previous teacher?

_____

_____

_____

pursuit

On a nature show, I watched a lion in **pursuit** of a zebra.

What might a house cat be in pursuit of?

_____

_____

Personification

Writers sometimes use words in unusual ways to help you better picture an animal, a thing, or an event. **Personification** gives human qualities to an animal or object.

 FIND TEXT EVIDENCE

When I read the sentence on page 133 "The sea will swallow you up!" I know the writer is using personification. The word swallow _gives the sea the action of a person._

"The sea will swallow you up!"

Your Turn The following sentence from "The Magical Lost Brocade" contains an example of personification. Explain how the example shows human qualities.

As he crossed the valley, angry flames leaped out at him, page 134 _____

_____

_____

Make Predictions

A prediction is a guess about what might happen. Making predictions helps you focus your reading. Use evidence from the story to see if your predictions are confirmed. If your predictions are not confirmed, you can correct them. This helps you check your understanding of the story.

 FIND TEXT EVIDENCE

After you read about the tasks Ping must do in order to find the brocade on page 134, you may want to predict whether or not he will succeed before you continue reading.

> **Quick Tip**
>
> Your predictions should make sense based on the story's genre. For example, folktales often have magical events. You may predict that Ping will find something magical that will help him during his journey.

Page 134

"It sounds like an extremely difficult journey," said Ping, "but I'll do my very best." He mounted the horse and traveled for three days, reaching the Fire Valley. As he crossed the valley, angry flames leaped out at him. The intense heat brought tears to Ping's eyes, but he said nothing.

When he reached the other side of the valley, he saw the Ice Ocean. With Ping's gentle **guidance**, the horse entered the frigid waters. The sea touched Ping with icy fingers, but he didn't shiver once. So horse and rider crossed the sea, **emerging** safely on the other side.

On page 134, Ping tells the old man, "It sounds like an extremely difficult journey, but I'll do my very best." I predicted Ping would succeed. As I continued reading, I saw my prediction was right.

Your Turn Tell one prediction you made after Ping left the Mountain of the Sun. Was your prediction correct? If not, tell how you revised it based on your knowledge of folktales. _____

_____

_____

_____

Setting

A **folktale** describes a hero's or heroine's quest or set of tasks he or she must accomplish. A folktale's setting is the distant past, and the cultural setting is often in a land specific to the people that created the story. It includes the repetition of actions or words and often includes foreshadowing and imagery.

Quick Tip

Sometimes words in a story do not give a full description of the setting. Looking at the illustrations can help you better understand the setting.

FIND TEXT EVIDENCE

I can tell that "The Magical Lost Brocade" is a folktale. It describes Ping's quest to find his mother's brocade, actions are repeated, and events are foreshadowed. The tale also contains imagery and is set long ago in China.

Page 133

Long ago, in China, a poor woman and her son, Ping, lived in a tiny hut. The woman earned a living weaving beautiful brocade hangings, which her son sold. She wished she could give Ping a better home, but alas, that was impossible. So she decided to weave a brocade of a magnificent house with gardens. At least they could look at something lovely. It took three years to complete the brocade, and it was her finest work. However, soon afterward, a great wind swept into their hut and carried it away! The woman was grief-stricken. So Ping went off in **pursuit** of the brocade, **assuring** his mother he would bring it home.

Ping walked for three days and came to a stone house. A bearded man sat outside. "I'm searching for my mother's brocade," Ping said.

"A brocade flew by three days ago," said the man. "Now it's in a palace far away. I'll explain how you can get there and lend you my horse." Ping thanked the man and bowed deeply to express his **gratitude**.

"First, you must ride through Fire Valley," said the man. "You must cross over it regardless of the scorching heat, without uttering a word. If you utter even a single sound, you'll burn!" He continued, "After you've crossed Fire Valley, you'll arrive at Ice Ocean. You must ride through the icy waters without shivering. If you shiver even once, the **outcome** will be terrible! The sea will swallow you up!" The old man paused before concluding, "When you emerge from the sea, you'll be facing the Mountain of the Sun. The mountain is as steep as a straight line up to the sky! The palace sits on top of the mountain, and the brocade is in the palace."

Setting
The story takes place long ago in China.

Foreshadowing
Foreshadowing gives readers clues about the outcome of events in a story.

Your Turn List two details that show "The Magical Lost Brocade" is a folktale. Then find examples that give clues about the cultural setting.

_____

_____

_____

_____

_____

Theme

The theme of a story is the big idea or message about life that the author wants to share. Usually, the theme is not stated directly. To identify the theme, think about the relationships of and conflicts among the characters. Many times, a reader can infer multiple themes in a story.

FIND TEXT EVIDENCE

When I read the end of the first paragraph of "The Magical Lost Brocade" on page 133, Ping makes a promise to his mother and sets off to keep it. I can use Ping's relationship with his mother to find the theme of the story.

Quick Tip

Each reader may infer a different theme. For example, one theme you may infer after reading the first paragraph on page 133 is, "Family members help each other." Make sure you use text evidence to infer a possible theme.

What Does the Character Do and Say?

> Ping promises his mother he will find her lost brocade and goes off to search for it.

What Happens to the Character?

> Ping goes on a three-day journey and meets a bearded man. The man gives Ping a plan to find the brocade.

Theme

> You should have a plan when you go in search of something.

Your Turn Reread "The Magical Lost Brocade." Complete the graphic organizer on page 141 to determine another theme of the story. Record what Ping does and says and the conflicts he faces. Then state the theme you inferred.

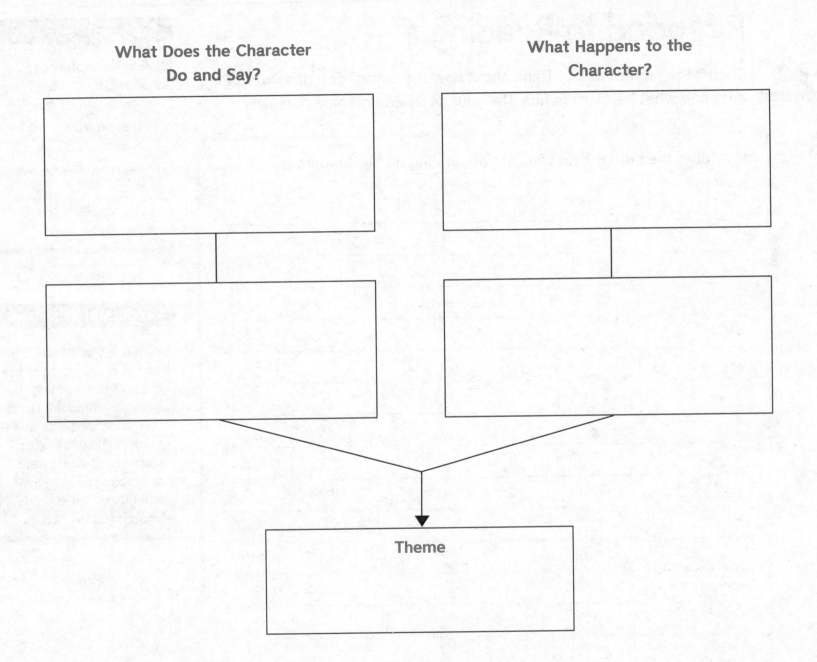

What Does the Character
Do and Say?

What Happens to the
Character?

Theme

Respond to Reading

COLLABORATE

Discuss the prompt below. Think about how the author describes what Ping does and what happens to him. Use your notes and graphic organizer.

How does the author help you care about Ping on his dangerous journey?

_____

_____

_____

_____

_____

_____

_____

_____

_____

_____

_____

_____

Research Plan

A plan can help to state a project's purpose and the steps needed to reach a goal or finish a product. Some features of a research plan are

- a list of materials
- steps, in logical order, to collect and record information
- observations made as steps are completed

Why is listing steps in logical order important for a research plan?

_____

_____

_____

Make an Illustrated Food Web With a partner, develop a plan for collecting information about a food web. A food web shows the flow of energy among producers, consumers, and decomposers. Include in your plan

- how you will gather information, such as observing things on a walk outdoors with an adult, using the library, or searching online with adult assistance
- jobs for each person, such as collecting and recording the information
- how you will present your food web

Arrange your findings in a food web illustrated with photos or drawings. Follow any oral instructions your partner may give to show that you understand them. After you finish, you will be sharing your work with the class.

Project: Illustrated Food Web

Materials: notebook, reference sources

Step 1: Arrange with a teacher for a walk outdoors.

What do you think would be a logical Step 2 for the above plan?

_____

_____

_____

Blancaflor

How does the author use personification to set the mood of the story?

Literature Anthology:
pages 118-131

Talk About It Reread **Literature Anthology** page 119. Turn to your partner and discuss how the author describes the tree.

Cite Text Evidence What phrases describe the tree and set the mood of the folktale? Write text evidence in the chart.

Evidence	Mood

 Evaluate Information

Authors use figurative language in folktales to create memorable stories. A simile compares things using *like* or *as*. A metaphor compares things without using *like* or *as*. Personification gives human qualities to nonhuman things. Why do you think it was appropriate or not for the author of this folktale to use personification?

Write The author uses personification to _____

_____

_____

How does the author use descriptive language to help you visualize what the prince is experiencing?

Talk About It Reread the first two paragraphs on **Literature Anthology** page 123. Talk to a partner about how the author describes the landscape and what happens to the prince.

Cite Text Evidence What phrases create imagery? Use this web to record text evidence.

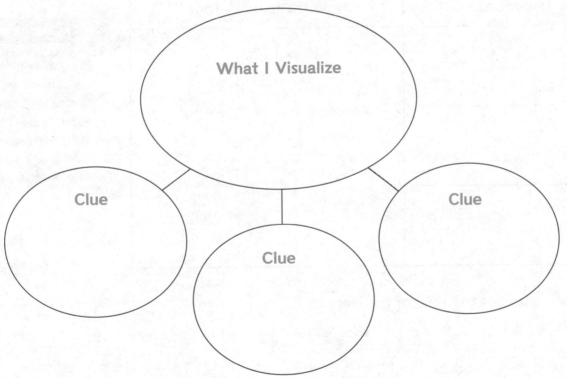

What I Visualize

Clue

Clue

Clue

Clue

Write I can visualize the setting because the author _____

_____

Quick Tip

The author uses phrases such as *deserted and barren* and *basalt and obsidian*. You can use context clues to help you understand what the phrases mean. For example, *deserted* describes a barren, or empty, place.

Evaluate Information

Details in the story can help you determine the setting. The setting can influence the plot. For example, a story set in a desert may have characters trying to find water in order to survive. How does the setting of *Blancaflor* affect what Alfonso does?

? **How does the author use words and phrases to change the tone of the story?**

Talk About It Reread paragraphs 3-6 on **Literature Anthology** page 130. Turn to a partner and discuss how the tone of the folktale changes.

Cite Text Evidence What phrases mark the climax, or turning point, of the story? Write them in the chart and how the tone changes.

Text Evidence	How It Changes Tone

Write The author changes the tone of the story by _____

_____

_____

Make Inferences

Blancaflor helps Alfonso in his conflict with her father. She tells Alfonso which horse to use to escape. Why does Alfonso choose the other horse instead?

Respond to Reading

COLLABORATE

Discuss the prompt below. Apply your knowledge of how folktales end to form your answer. Use your notes and graphic organizer.

Think about how the author uses figurative language. How does the tone and mood change from the beginning of the folktale to the end?

_____

_____

_____

_____

_____

_____

_____

_____

_____

_____

_____

Quick Tip

Use these sentence starters to paraphrase the text and to help organize your text evidence.

- *The author sets the tone by . . .*

- *The author uses figurative language to show . . .*

- *The mood changes because . . .*

Self-Selected Reading

Choose a text to read independently and fill in your writer's notebook with the title, author, and genre. Record your purpose for reading. For example, you may be reading to answer a question or for entertainment.

From Tale to Table

Literature Anthology:
pages 134–137

1   Whether it's a princess turning into a dove or a frog turning into a prince, many folktales and fairy tales include a magical transformation of one thing into another. Though it seems like an impossible task that only a magician could do, transformations can in fact happen in real life—even in your own kitchen!

A Wise Plan

2   Through the process of cooking and baking, individual ingredients can be transformed into something delicious. Did you know that the bread in the sandwich you had for lunch was probably made with only six basic ingredients: flour, water, oil, yeast, salt, and sugar? It may seem impossible, but by combining and heating these ingredients you can create something different: bread. It's not magic, but it does require a plan.

Reread paragraph 1. **Circle** clues that show what the author does to help you understand what a transformation is. Then **underline** what the author thinks of transformations. Write it here:

_____

_____

_____

COLLABORATE

Reread paragraph 2. Talk with your partner about what you have to do to transform ingredients into bread. **Write** the numbers 1 to 6 beside each ingredient.

Then **draw a box** around what the author uses to foreshadow what information comes next.

(bkgd) Dave King/Dorling Kindersley/Getty Images

Too Hot, Too Cold, and Just Right

1   A recipe has usually been tried and tested previously, so it is important to follow the steps carefully to get the same result. Slight changes in temperature can affect the outcome. For example, in step 1, the water should be warm, not hot. Why? Though it's hard to tell by looking at it, yeast is a living organism. At the right temperature, it gives off gases that create bubbles in the dough. This is what makes the dough rise. If you use hot water in the recipe, you can kill the yeast. If you use cold water, the yeast may create very little or no gas. Without the gas that the yeast produces, the dough will not rise.

Reread the excerpt. **Underline** what the author thinks is important to do when using a recipe. **Circle** something that might happen if you don't do it.

COLLABORATE

Talk with a partner about how the author uses cause and effect to organize information. Illustrate with **a mark** in the margin beside each cause-and-effect relationship in the paragraph. Write one of them here:

_____

_____

_____

_____

? **Why is "From Tale to Table" a good title for this selection?**

Talk About It Reread paragraph 1 on page 148. Talk with a partner about how the author introduces the selection and why that introduction is important.

Cite Text Evidence How does the author connect tales and recipes? Write text evidence in the chart.

Synthesize Information

Combine what you know about folktales with information in "From Tale to Table." Why does the author of "From Tale to Table" use "magical transformation" in the introduction?

```
┌─────────────────────────────┐
│                             │
└──────────────┬──────────────┘
               ↓
┌─────────────────────────────┐
│                             │
└──────────────┬──────────────┘
               ↓
┌─────────────────────────────┐
│                             │
└──────────────┬──────────────┘
               ↓
┌─────────────────────────────┐
│                             │
└─────────────────────────────┘
```

Write "From Tale to Table" is a good title for this selection because _____

_____

_____

TADDEUS/Shutterstock.com

Logical Order

Text structure includes the way an author organizes information or ideas for the readers. An author of a procedure or process may use an organizational pattern such as order of importance or logical order.

FIND TEXT EVIDENCE

In the second paragraph of "From Tale to Table" on page 148, the author discusses the process of cooking and baking. The author organizes the text in a logical order by giving an example of bread and stating that the process begins with the ingredients.

> Did you know that the bread in the sandwich you had for lunch was probably made with only six basic ingredients: flour, water, oil, yeast, salt, and sugar?

Your Turn Reread the text on page 149 in the section "Too Hot, Too Cold, and Just Right."

- In this section, how does the author organize the text in a logical order?

_____

_____

- Why does this organizational pattern make sense? _____

_____

_____

COLLABORATE

Readers to Writers

When writing a text about a process, take the time to plan a logical order of steps you feel are important. Then note the most important ideas you want readers to know about each step.

Text Connections

Library of Congress Prints and Photographs Division [LC-USZ62-127779]

? **How do the Wright brothers and the authors of *Blancaflor* and "From Tale to Table" help you understand how plans can help people accomplish a task?**

Talk About It Look at the sketches and read the caption. Talk with a partner about each image and what they tell you about the Wright brothers.

Cite Text Evidence Circle three things in the sketches that show how the Wright brothers planned to build their flying machine. Think about why the Wright brothers drew up these plans. In the margin beside each sketch, write words that describe the plans.

Write The Wright brothers and the authors show

_____

_____

_____

_____

_____

_____

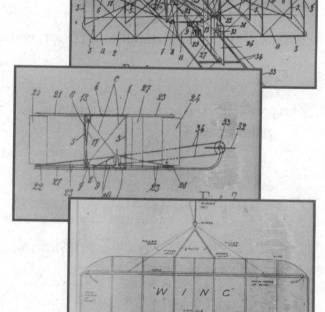

The Wright brothers drew up these plans for their flying machine in 1908.

Present Your Work

Discuss with your partner how you will present your plan and illustrated food web. Use the Listening Checklist as your classmates give their presentations. Discuss the sentence starters below and write your answers.

I learned that a research plan should _____

_____

_____

The most important step in developing a plan is _____

_____

_____

Quick Tip

Decide on the roles each person will have during the presentation. Rehearse with your partner and follow all the instructions you agree upon. Be prepared to answer any questions from your audience.

✓ Listening Checklist

☐ Listen actively by taking notes on the presenter's ideas.

☐ Pay attention to verbal messages and nonverbal messages, such as pointing to parts of the web.

☐ Ask relevant questions, such as asking about parts of the plan.

☐ Make pertinent, or relevant, comments, such as what you liked about the presentation.

Talk About It

Essential Question

What motivates you to accomplish a goal?

154   Unit 2 • Poetry

COLLABORATE

Goals keep us focused. Look at the photo. Talk about what you see. These ambitious dancers will have to rehearse for hours each day if they want the satisfaction of reaching their goal of being great dancers.

When you set a goal for yourself, what does it take to achieve it? How will you know you have accomplished your goal? Write your ideas in the web.

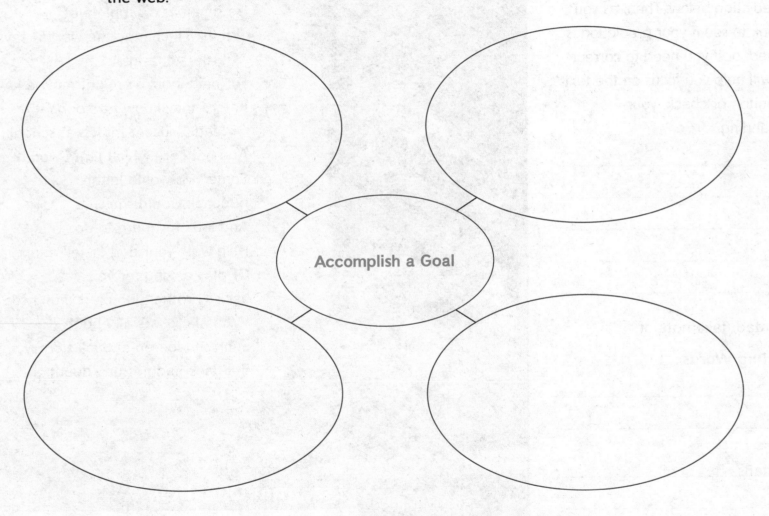

Accomplish a Goal

BLAST BACK! studysync

Go online to **my.mheducation.com** and read the "Reaching a Goal" Blast. When was the last time you had a goal that you tried to reach? Did you reach it? How did you know when you had reached your goal? Then blast back your response.

Ruth Jenkinson/Dorling Kindersley/Getty Images

TAKE NOTES

Use the photos and titles to predict what the poem will be about. Write your prediction below. Then, as you read, look to see if your prediction is confirmed, or if you need to correct it. This will help you focus on the text and monitor, or check, your understanding.

_____

_____

_____

_____

As you read, take note of:

Interesting Words _____

_____

_____

Key Details _____

_____

_____

_____

_____

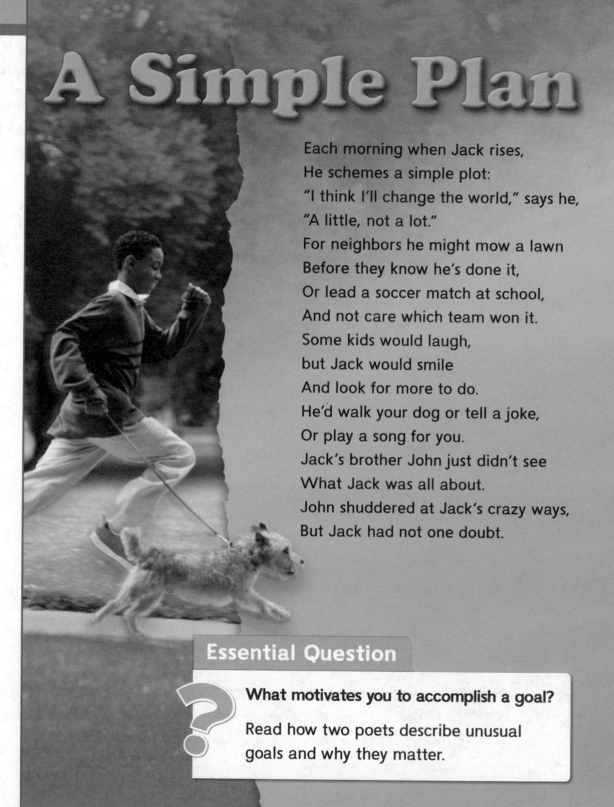

A Simple Plan

Each morning when Jack rises,
He schemes a simple plot:
"I think I'll change the world," says he,
"A little, not a lot."
For neighbors he might mow a lawn
Before they know he's done it,
Or lead a soccer match at school,
And not care which team won it.
Some kids would laugh,
but Jack would smile
And look for more to do.
He'd walk your dog or tell a joke,
Or play a song for you.
Jack's brother John just didn't see
What Jack was all about.
John shuddered at Jack's crazy ways,
But Jack had not one doubt.

Essential Question

? **What motivates you to accomplish a goal?**

Read how two poets describe unusual goals and why they matter.

"Who wants to do another's chores?"
John asked. "What does it mean,
'I'll change the world?' You're wasting time.
What changes have you seen?"
"Little brother," Jack explained,
"I used to think like you.
I thought, 'Why bother?' and 'Who cares?'
I see you do that, too.
I'd see some grass not mowed, or else
Kids not getting along,
And in the park no games to play—
I'd wonder what was wrong.
And then I had to ask myself,
What was I waiting for?
The change can start with me, you see,
That key is in my door.
I've memorized a thousand names,
And everyone knows me.
What do *you* do?" John had to think.
And he began to see.
Now each morning when Jack rises,
He hears his brother plan:
"I think I'll change the world," says John,
"If I can't, then who can?"

— Peter Collier

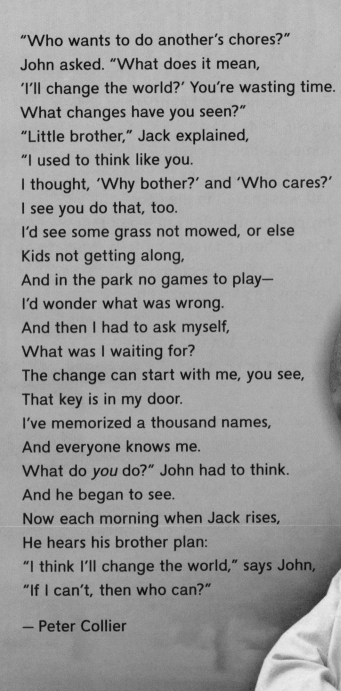

(l) Peter Zander/Workbook Stock/Getty Images; (r) Fancy/Alamy

FIND TEXT EVIDENCE 🔍

Read

Page 156–157

Repetition

Draw a box around the words *I'll change the world*. Who says this the first time? Who says it the second time? Who says it the last time?

_____

_____

_____

Page 157

Theme

By the end of the poem, what lesson has John learned? **Underline** the text evidence.

_____

_____

_____

Reread

Author's Craft

How does the repetition in this poem help create a theme?

FIND TEXT EVIDENCE 🔍

Read

Page 158

Homographs

Circle the context clues that help you determine the meaning of the word *tipped*. Write the meaning.

_____

Page 158

Theme

Underline details about the effect of the oil spill on the birds. What do they tell you about how the speaker feels?

_____
_____
_____
_____
_____
_____

Reread

Author's Craft

How does the poet help you visualize the effect of the spill?

RESCUE

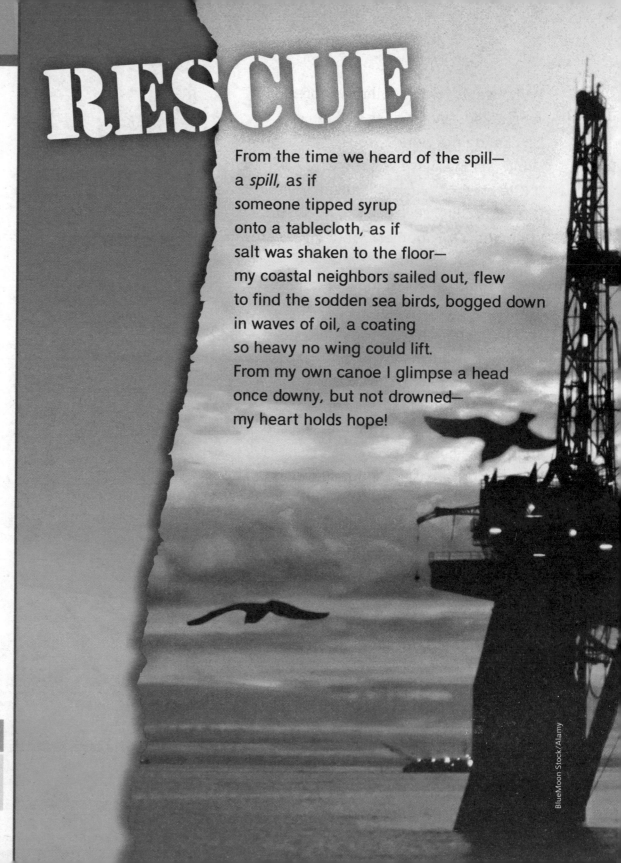

From the time we heard of the spill—
a *spill*, as if
someone tipped syrup
onto a tablecloth, as if
salt was shaken to the floor—
my coastal neighbors sailed out, flew
to find the sodden sea birds, bogged down
in waves of oil, a coating
so heavy no wing could lift.
From my own canoe I glimpse a head
once downy, but not drowned—
my heart holds hope!

BlueMoon Stock/Alamy

Reach, lift, and up—
it beats, this bird's heart!
I hold the sickened seagull, know:
Just as one spill can spell disaster,
One boat can bring back life.

— Elena Ruiz

Make Connections

Compare the speakers' feelings in the poems to the feelings you have when you try to accomplish a goal.

Talk about whether your prediction on page 156 was confirmed.

FIND TEXT EVIDENCE

Read

Page 159

Free Verse

Free verse poems don't group words by rhyme. They group words to emphasize meaning. **Underline** the first line. What might the speaker be emphasizing?

_____

_____

_____

Theme

Draw a box around the last two lines on page 159. What is a meaning of these lines?

_____

_____

_____

Reread

Author's Craft

How would the poem be different if the speaker had told about the spill as an observer instead of a rescuer?

Vocabulary

Use the example sentences to talk with a partner about each word. Then answer the questions.

ambitious

Paulo is an **ambitious** bike rider and always looks for challenges.

What makes someone ambitious?

_____

_____

memorized

Pat **memorized** the poem and recited it perfectly for the class.

What is the name of a poem or song that you memorized?

_____

_____

satisfaction

Participating in sports, such as basketball, gave Jason great **satisfaction**.

What activity gives you great satisfaction?

_____

_____

shuddered

Jill **shuddered** as she bit into the tart, juicy lemon.

What is a synonym for shuddered?

_____

_____

Poetry Terms

narrative

I like to read **narrative** poems because they tell a story.

What story would you like to tell in a narrative poem?

_____

_____

repetition

The **repetition** of words, phrases, or lines is used for emphasis.

What is the repetition of a word or phrase that you would use to emphasize happiness?

_____

_____

free verse

A **free verse** poem does not have a set rhyming patterns.

What topic would you choose for a free verse poem?

_____

_____

rhyme

A poem with **rhyme** contains words that end with the same sound.

Can you think of three words that rhyme with *funny*?

_____

_____

_____

> **Build Your Word List** Reread "Rescue" on pages 158–159. Underline three adjectives. In your writer's notebook, write the three words. Use an online or print thesaurus to find two synonyms for each word. Write the synonyms next to each adjective.

Homographs

Homographs are words that are spelled the same but have different meanings and may or may not have the same pronunciation. You can use context clues to help figure out which meaning is correct.

🔍 FIND TEXT EVIDENCE

In "A Simple Plan," I see the word park. *I know that* park *can be a verb meaning "to place or leave something" and it can also be a noun meaning "land set apart for recreation." The phrase "games to play" is a clue that* park *has the second meaning.*

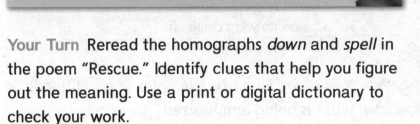

I'd see some grass not mowed, or else
Kids not getting along,
And in the park no games to play—
I'd wonder what was wrong.

Your Turn Reread the homographs *down* and *spell* in the poem "Rescue." Identify clues that help you figure out the meaning. Use a print or digital dictionary to check your work.

_____

_____

_____

Repetition and Rhyme

Quick Tip

Words that rhyme don't always end with the same spelling. To hear and identify the rhyming words, try reading the poem out loud. Reading aloud will also help you hear a rhyming pattern.

Poets may use **repetition**, or the repeated use of words, sounds, or phrases, for effect. Repeating a word, phrase, or sentence style helps emphasize the meaning. Words **rhyme** when their endings sound the same.

FIND TEXT EVIDENCE

Reread the poem "Rescue" on pages 158 and 159. Look for phrases and words that are repeated and the effect they create.

Page 158

From the time we heard of the spill—
a *spill*, as if
someone tipped syrup
onto a tablecloth, as if
salt was shaken to the floor—
my coastal neighbors sailed out, flew
to find the sodden sea birds, bogged down
in waves of oil, a coating
so heavy no wing could lift.

The word "spill" is repeated to emphasize the event. The words "as if" are repeated to emphasize that the spill in the poem is worse than spilling syrup or salt.

Your Turn Find two examples of repetition in "A Simple Plan" and tell what is being emphasized.

1 _____

_____

2 _____

_____

Narrative and Free Verse

Narrative poetry tells a story. It has characters and can have dialogue. Narrative poetry can rhyme but does not have to.

Free verse shares ideas and feelings with no set rhyming pattern or rhythm. It has no set line length.

 FIND TEXT EVIDENCE

I can tell that "A Simple Plan" is a narrative poem because it tells a story and has dialogue between characters. I see that "Rescue" is free verse because there is no set line length or rhyming pattern.

Readers to Writers

The narrator, or the voice that you hear in the poem, is called the *speaker*. The poet is the *writer* of the poem. Details tell you what the speaker is feeling or thinking. When writing about a poem, make sure to distinguish between the speaker and the poet.

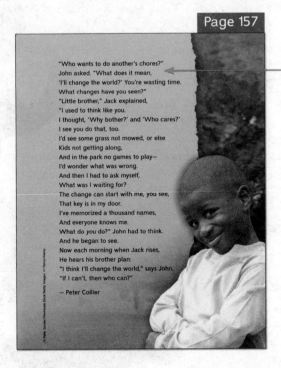

Page 157

"Who wants to do another's chores?"
John asked. "What does it mean,
'I'll change the world?' You're wasting time.
What changes have you seen?"
"Little brother," Jack explained,
"I used to think like you.
I thought, 'Why bother?' and 'Who cares?'
I see you do that, too.
I'd see some grass not mowed, or else
Kids not getting along,
And in the park no games to play—
I'd wonder what was wrong.
And then I had to ask myself,
What was I waiting for?
The change can start with me, you see,
That key is in my door.
I've memorized a thousand names,
And everyone knows me.
What do *you* do?" John had to think.
And he began to see.
Now each morning when Jack rises,
He hears his brother plan:
"I think I'll change the world," says John,
"If I can't, then who can?"

— Peter Collier

"A Simple Plan" is a narrative poem because it tells a story, has characters, and includes dialogue. Like some narrative poems, this one also rhymes.

 Your Turn Reread the poems "A Simple Plan" and "Rescue." How does the choice to rhyme or not to rhyme affect the poems?

_____

_____

_____

_____

Theme

The **theme** is the big idea or message that the poet wishes to communicate. Thinking about the speaker, word choices, and key details that the poet uses can help you figure out the theme of the poem.

🔍 **FIND TEXT EVIDENCE**

Both poems are about accomplishing goals, but each poem has a specific theme. I'll reread "A Simple Plan," think about who is speaking, and look for key details to figure out the poem's theme.

Quick Tip

To find the theme in a poem that tells a story, you can ask: "What lesson does the character or speaker learn in this poem?"

Detail
"I think I'll change the world"

↓

Detail
I thought, 'Why bother?'

↓

Detail
The change can start with me.

↓

Theme
Helping to make the world better gives life purpose and meaning.

Your Turn Reread the poem "Rescue." Think about the speaker and list key details in the graphic organizer on page 165. Use the key details to figure out the theme of the poem.

Peter Zander/Workbook Stock/Getty Images

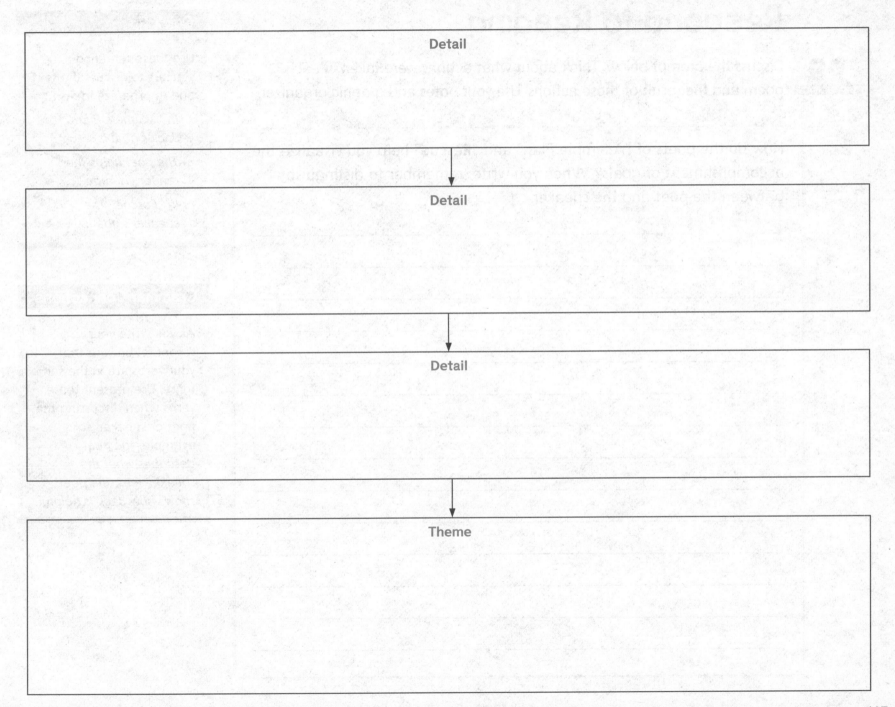

Detail

Detail

Detail

Theme

Respond to Reading

COLLABORATE

Discuss the prompt below. Think about what actions were taken in each poem and the result of those actions. Use your notes and graphic organizer.

How do the poets of "A Simple Plan" and "Rescue" help you visualize the accomplishment of goals? When you write, remember to distinguish between the poet and the speaker.

_____

_____

_____

_____

_____

_____

_____

_____

_____

_____

_____

_____

Quick Tip

Use these sentence starters to discuss the text and to organize ideas.

- In "A Simple Plan," Jack's goal is . . .
- The poet helps the reader visualize . . .
- In "Rescue," the speaker's goal is . . .

Grammar Connections

As you write your response, be sure that your verbs are in the same tense. Use present tense verbs when discussing the poet or speaker, for example, *the poet* **describes** *what the speaker* **sees**; *the poet* **shows** *how Jack* **is helpful**.

Figurative Language

Authors use **figurative language** to create mental images in the reader's mind and to deepen understanding. Figurative language includes

- simile and metaphor. A simile makes a comparison using the words *like* or *as*. A metaphor makes a comparison without using *like* or *as*.
- personification, or giving human qualities to non-human things.
- hyperbole, or exaggeration not meant to be taken literally.

How can figurative language help readers better understand an author's ideas?

_____

_____

Create an Illustration With a partner, research historical poems about the Founding Fathers and patriot heroes. Ask an adult to help you follow a research plan. For example, a librarian can help you find books with historical poems or choose key words for an online search. Select and analyze a poem for the following

- types of figurative language
- mental images and meanings created by the figurative language

Use your information to create an illustration for your poem. You and your partner can each create an illustration. The illustrations can be done digitally or by hand. After you complete your illustration, you will present your work to the class.

From "Paul Revere's Ride" by Henry Wadsworth Longfellow

A phantom ship, with each mast and spar
Across the moon like a prison bar

In the two lines of poetry above, from the historical poem about the patriot Paul Revere, Henry Wadsworth Longfellow uses a simile to compare each mast and spar of the ship to a prison bar.

Longfellow, Henry Wadsworth. Paul Revere's Ride. (1863). Boston, Massachusetts: Project Gutenberg. Retrieved June 12, 2017, from http://www.gutenberg.org/ebooks/25153

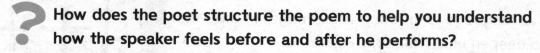

Stage Fright

 How does the poet structure the poem to help you understand how the speaker feels before and after he performs?

*Literature Anthology:
pages 138–140*

COLLABORATE

Talk About It Reread pages 138–139 in the **Literature Anthology.** Talk to your partner about how the poet sets the lines of the poem and how they relate to how the speaker feels.

Cite Text Evidence What does the poet write to help you visualize what the speaker is feeling? Write text evidence in the chart.

✂ Evaluate Information

Notice the way the structure and appearance of the poem changes in the middle and at the end. How do these sections relate to each other?

What the Poet Writes	What I Visualize

Write The poet helps me understand how the speaker feels by _____

_____

_____

_____

Catching Quiet

? **Why does the poet use repetition in "Catching Quiet"?**

Talk About It Reread page 140 in the **Literature Anthology**. Turn to your partner and discuss the words and phrases the poet repeats.

Cite Text Evidence What words and phrases are repeated? Cite text evidence and explain why the poet repeats them.

Words and Phrases	Author's Purpose

Write The poet uses repetition in "Catching Quiet" to _____

_____

_____

_____

Quick Tip

There can be many different ideas about the purpose of a phrase or line in a poem. As long as there is text evidence to support an idea, there may be a variety of correct responses when discussing poetry.

Respond to Reading

COLLABORATE

Discuss the prompt below. Apply your knowledge of poetry to inform your answer. Use your notes and graphic organizer.

Think about the way both poems are organized. How do techniques like line arrangement and repetition help convey each poem's theme?

_____

_____

_____

_____

_____

_____

_____

_____

_____

_____

_____

_____

_____

_____

_____

Foul Shot

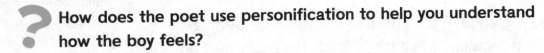

? **How does the poet use personification to help you understand how the boy feels?**

Literature Anthology:
pages 142–143

Talk About It Reread page 142 in the **Literature Anthology**. Turn to your partner and talk about how the poet describes what the boy is feeling.

Cite Text Evidence What words and phrases help you create mental images of how the boy feels? Write text evidence in the chart.

Quick Tip

Use the word *person* in "personification" to help you remember meaning. *Personification* means giving human qualities to an animal or object.

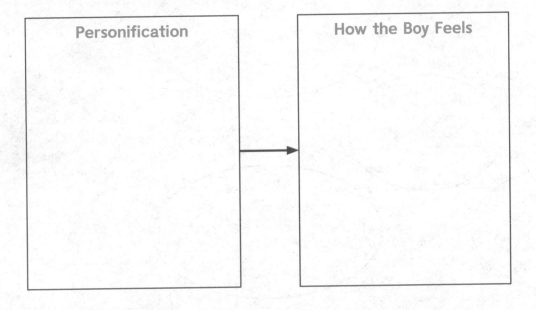

Personification	How the Boy Feels

Write The poet uses personification to help me understand _____

_____

_____

How does the poet's word choice create suspense in "Foul Shot"?

COLLABORATE

Talk About It Reread page 143 in the **Literature Anthology**. With a partner, talk about what happens when the boy lets the basketball go.

Cite Text Evidence What words and phrases create a feeling of suspense in the poem? Write text evidence in the web.

> **Quick Tip**
>
> Reading the poem out loud with expression will help you hear the words and phrases that create suspense.

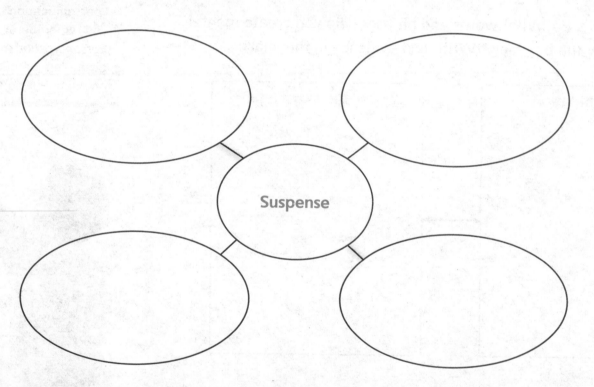

Suspense

Write The poet creates suspense by using words and phrases to _____
_____
_____

Voice

In poetry, the voice telling the poem belongs to the speaker. Voice gives the speaker a specific personality. Voice is created through the poet's use of language. The poet can use voice to show how the speaker feels. For example, the words the poet chooses can make the voice in the poem sound happy, sad, excited, energetic, or lonely.

 FIND TEXT EVIDENCE

Read aloud "Foul Shot" on pages 142–143 in the **Literature Anthology**. Think about how the speaker describes what is happening. On page 143, many of the lines have only one word. This stretches out the moments before the ball drops, creating suspense. The voice in these lines sounds very excited and focused on the game.

Your Turn Reread lines 11–13 lines on page 143.

- How are these lines different than the rest of the poem? _____

_____

_____

_____

- How do these lines contribute to the voice in the poem? _____

_____

_____

_____

Readers to Writers

Think about how the speaker in the poem is feeling. When writing your own poem, choose words, line lengths, and sentence structures that will best convey the speaker's feelings.

Text Connections

? How do the photographer and poets of "Stage Fright" and "Foul Shot" show how crowds or audiences affect performance?

COLLABORATE

Talk About It Look at the photograph and read the caption. With a partner, discuss whether you think the crowd affects the way Althea Gibson plays tennis.

Cite Text Evidence **Underline** clues in the photograph that show what might affect Althea Gibson as she plays tennis. **Circle** details that show how she feels.

Write I can see how a crowd can affect performance because the photographer and poets _____

_____

_____

_____

_____

Popperfoto/Getty Images

Althea Gibson was the first African-American tennis player to compete at Wimbledon. She won in 1957 and 1958.

> **Quick Tip**
>
> Picture the audience in the poems "Stage Fright" and "Foul Shot." Compare them to the crowd watching Althea Gibson in the photo. What do they all have in common? You can use these words when you are making a comparison: *alike, and, both, similiar, same.*

Expression and Phrasing

Think about the meaning of the poem when you read aloud. Reading a poem with *expression* makes it more interesting and makes the ideas in the poem clearer. Commas, dashes, and other punctuation marks indicate *phrasing*, or when to pause while reading. Reading with good expression and phrasing, or prosody, can also make the poem's meaning clearer.

Page 158

Reach, lift, and up —
It beats, this bird's heart!
I hold the sickened seagull, know:
Just as one spill can spell disaster,
One boat can bring back life

The dashes in this poem signal places to pause while reading.

Your Turn Turn back to pages 158 and 159. Take turns reading aloud "Rescue" with a partner. Pay attention to punctuation. Visualize what is happening in the poem. How does the poet want the reader to feel? Express your feelings in the way you read the poem.

Afterward, think about how you did. Complete these sentences.

I remembered to _____

_____

Next time, I will _____

_____

Literature Anthology:
pages 138–139

Expert Model

Features of a Narrative Poem

A narrative poem is a type of poem that tells a story. A narrative poem

- often contains sensory language, or words that appeal to the senses

- usually includes both concrete words and figurative language

- tells a story in verse form and may contain characters, setting, and plot events

Word Wise

Notice that some sentences are broken up into different lines. This focuses the reader on the image or feeling in each part of the sentence. For example: "I studied and studied/my perfect Prince-part" focuses the reader first on how hard the speaker worked, and then focuses on his feelings about the part in the play.

Analyze an Expert Model Studying other narrative poems will help you learn how to plan and write a narrative poem of your own. **Reread** "Stage Fright" on pages 138 and 139 in the **Literature Anthology**. Write your answers to the questions below.

Give two examples of sensory language from "Stage Fright." Why do you think the poet chose this language? _____

_____

_____

The climax of a narrative is part of the plot. The climax is the turning point or the highest point of interest and suspense in the narrative. What is the climax of the poem? How is the situation resolved? _____

_____

_____

Plan: Choose Your Topic

Freewrite Think about postive things you have accomplished. What are you proud of having done? Maybe you got a good grade on a test, learned to do something well, or helped raise money for a good cause. Quickly write your ideas without stopping. Then discuss your ideas with a partner.

Quick Tip

Remember that narrative poems tell stories. Think about how your details are important to the story. Ask yourself: What do the details help the reader understand?

_____

_____

_____

_____

_____

Writing Prompt Write a narrative poem about one of your achievements.

I will write about _____

Purpose and Audience Think about who will read or hear your poem. Will your purpose be to inform, persuade, or entertain them?

My purpose for writing a narrative poem is to _____

The audience will be _____

The language I will use in my poem will be _____

Plan In your writer's notebook, make a Details web that lists some of the details you will include in your poem. Fill in at least two details.

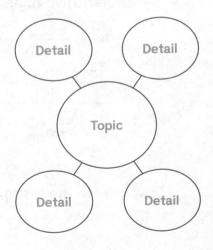

Plan: Sensory Language

Brainstorm Descriptive Details Once you have chosen some details you plan to include in your poem, think how to best describe them. One way to describe details is by using sensory language, which are words that appeal to the five senses (taste, touch, sight, smell, and hearing). Be descriptive when using sensory language. For example, "we ran through the soft green grass" helps the reader understand the speaker's experience more than just "we ran through the grass." As you plan your first draft, ask yourself these questions:

- Will my readers understand the details I have included?

- Are the words I'm using related to any of the five senses?

- Do I need to use more descriptive sensory language to help the reader better visualize what is happening?

Think of two lines containing descriptive details you might use in your narrative poem. Appeal to two different senses.

1 _____

_____

2 _____

_____

Graphic Organizer Once you've decided on all the details you will include, fill in the rest of your Details web. If you need more space to write your details, use a separate sheet of paper in your writer's notebook.

Draft

Figurative Language Poets often use figurative language to help readers create mental images and deepen understanding. Figurative language includes metaphor, simile, personification, and hyperbole. Read the lines below. In the poem, a metaphor is used to compare making a change with a key in a door.

> And then I had to ask myself,
>
> What was I waiting for?
>
> The change can start with me, you see,
>
> That key is in my door.

Now use the lines above as a model to write lines that might be included in your narrative poem. Include an example of figurative language.

_____

_____

_____

_____

Write a Draft Use your Details web to help you write your draft in your writer's notebook. Use sensory and figurative language in your poem. Remember that your poem is telling a story and should include plot events. Check that your narrative poem tells a story and has a beginning, middle, and end.

Word Wise

A simile compares two things by using the words *like* or *as*; for example, *the song was like an old friend greeting me.* A metaphor is a direct comparison that refers to one thing as another, but does not use the words *like* or *as*; for example, *the song was an old friend greeting me.*

WRITING

Revise

Concrete Words One way poets can create mental images for readers is to use concrete words instead of, or in addition to, abstract ones. Concrete words name things we can know through our senses, like "red," "hot," and "car." Abstract words refer to ideas and concepts, like "kindness" and "excitement." Read the lines below. Then revise them so they contain more concrete words and create stronger images. The more specific and precise you can be, the better.

Quick Tip

Close your eyes while a friend reads your draft to you. Do the words help you accurately visualize what is happening? What concrete words can you add to better help your reader understand the feelings and actions in the poem?

> When I sat down at the piano, I felt so nervous.
>
> But as soon as I started to play, I became calm.

 Revision Revise your draft. Check that you have used enough sensory details, figurative language, and concrete words to help your reader really understand your experience.

Tetra Images - Daniel Grill/Brand X Pictures/Getty Images

Peer Conferences

COLLABORATE

Review a Draft Listen carefully as a partner reads his or her work aloud. Take notes about what you liked and what was difficult to follow. Begin by telling what you liked about the draft. Ask questions that will help the writer think more about the writing. Make suggestions that you think will make the writing stronger. Use these sentence starters.

I enjoyed this part of your draft because . . .

More concrete words or sensory language would help me visualize . . .

I have a question about . . .

This part is unclear to me. Can you explain why . . .

Partner Feedback After your partner gives you feedback on your draft, write one of the suggestions that you will use in your revision. Refer to the rubric on page 183 as you give feedback.

Based on my partner's feedback, I will _____

_____

_____

_____

After you finish giving each other feedback, reflect on the peer conference. What was helpful? What might you do differently next time?

Revision As you revise your draft use the Revising Checklist to help you figure out what text you may need to move, elaborate on, or delete. Remember to use the rubric on page 183 to help you with your revision.

Revising Checklist

☑ Revising Checklist

☐ Does my poem tell a story?

☐ What details can I add, subtract, combine, or rearrange to make my poem clearer?

☐ Do I use enough sensory and figurative language to help readers fully visualize the story?

☐ Are there places where additional concrete words would improve my poem?

Edit and Proofread

When you **edit** and **proofread** your writing, you look for and correct mistakes in spelling, punctuation, capitalization, and grammar. Reading through a revised draft multiple times can help you make sure you're catching any errors. Use the checklist below to edit your sentences.

Grammar Connections

Use *more, better,* and *worse* to compare two people, places, or things. Use *most, best,* and *worst* to compare more than two people, places, or things.

✔ Editing Checklist

☐ If you used dialogue, are quotation marks used correctly?

☐ Are all prepositional phrases used correctly?

☐ Are proper nouns capitalized?

☐ Are descriptive adjectives used correctly, including comparative and superlative forms?

☐ Are all words spelled correctly?

List two mistakes you found as you proofread your narrative poem.

1 _____

_____

2 _____

_____

Publish, Present, and Evaluate

Publishing When you **publish** your writing, you create a clean, neat final copy that is free of mistakes. As you write your final draft be sure to write legibly in cursive. Check that you are holding your pencil or pen correctly and are correctly spacing words.

Presentation When you are ready to **present** your work, rehearse your presentation. Use the Presenting Checklist to help you.

Evaluate After you publish your writing, use the rubric below to **evaluate** your writing.

What did you do successfully? _____

What needs more work? _____

_____

✓ **Presenting Checklist**

☐ Look out at the audience and make eye contact. Connecting with the audience helps them stay interested.

☐ Speak clearly and with expression.

☐ Make sure your reading rate matches the feelings you are describing.

☐ Use natural gestures and appropriate volume as you speak.

4	3	2	1
• the poem clearly tells a narrative, or story, about a time the writer accomplished a goal • effectively uses sensory language and concrete words to create a picture in the reader's mind • effectively uses figurative language	• the poem tells a narrative, or story, about a time the writer accomplished a goal • some sensory language and concrete words are used to create a picture in the reader's mind • some figurative language is used	• the poem tells a narrative, or story • uses little sensory language and few concrete words to create a picture in a reader's mind • very little figurative language is used	• the poem does not tell a narrative, or story • does not use any sensory language or enough concrete words to create a clear picture in the reader's mind • no figurative language is used

◎ Spiral Review

You have learned new skills and strategies in Unit 2 that will help you read more critically. Now it is time to practice what you have learned.

- **Context Clues**
- **Headings**
- **Make Inferences**
- **Personification**
- **Problem and Solution**
- **Theme**

Connect to Content

- **Write an Ad**
- **Make a Timeline**
- **"The Long Road"**

Read the selection and choose the best answer to each question.

Searching for FREEDOM

[1] In England in the 1600s, it was illegal to belong to any church except the Church of England. Those who spoke out against the church faced persecution, or harsh treatment for their religious beliefs. One group that spoke out against the church were the Pilgrims. A pilgrim is someone who makes a journey for religious reasons. Believing that the Church of England would never make the changes they wanted, the Pilgrims decided to head for North America.

[2] Another group that disagreed with the Church of England were the Puritans. The Puritans also wanted to reform the Church of England. Like the Pilgrims, the Puritans were persecuted for their religious beliefs. Many faced jail, threats, and other difficulties. Many Puritans also crossed the Atlantic Ocean in search of religious freedom.

A Debt Repaid

[3] William Penn came from a wealthy and powerful English family that belonged to the Church of England. Penn, however, joined another religious group called the Quakers. The Quakers were <u>tolerant</u> of other religions. They believed everyone was equal. Like the Pilgrims and other religious groups, the Quakers were persecuted in England.

[4] Penn's father had loaned money to King Charles II. When his father died, Penn asked the king to repay this debt with land in North America. The king gave him a large piece of land located west of New Jersey and southwest of New York. Penn called it Pennsylvania, which means "Penn's Woods." He founded a colony where Quakers—and everyone else—could worship freely.

Peace and Diversity

[5] Unlike many other European settlers, William Penn dealt fairly with Native Americans. He signed a peace treaty with the Lenni Lenape tribe, and paid them for their lands. Penn welcomed Native American refugees from other colonies, too. Because of this, the colony was peaceful for a very long time.

[6] William Penn's primary motivation for founding Pennsylvania was religious freedom. From its earliest days, Pennsylvania welcomed ethnic and religious diversity. Diversity means having people who are different in some way living or working together in the same place. The name Penn chose for the first capital of Pennsylvania reflects his Quaker beliefs. He called it Philadelphia, which means "city of brotherly love."

Popperfoto/Getty Images

1 The author uses a problem and solution text structure to —

    A explain how some groups dealt with religious persecution

    B illustrate what happened when people went to North America

    C describe problems caused by followers of the Church of England

    D encourage the reader to think of different ways to solve problems

2 Which words in paragraph 3 help the reader understand what <u>tolerant</u> means?

    F wealthy and powerful

    G joined another religious group

    H believed everyone was equal

    J persecuted in England

3 The author uses subheadings to help the reader understand —

    A some problems of English religions in the 1600s

    B how and why William Penn founded Pennsylvania

    C when Philadelphia became a city of brotherly love

    D discrimination and persecution in North America

> **Quick Tip**
>
> Think about the subheads. Then reread paragraphs 4 and 6. Which answer choice does the text evidence best support?

4 Based on information in the selection, what can the reader infer about the Pilgrims, the Puritans, and the Quakers?

    F They were loyal members of the Church of England.

    G They had to leave England to follow their religious beliefs.

    H They wanted to establish new territories for the king.

    J They joined together to create a new church in the colonies.

Read the poem and choose the best answer to each question.

ZIGGY

My uncle moved to another country
And gave us Ziggy, his big friendly dog with
hair as black as coal, long droopy ears,
a wagging tail and the habit of

5   doing what he wanted with a big crooked doggy smile.

I shouted, "Ziggy, come here!" every day as
he ran toward the waiting hills and tangled woods
behind our house. But he always kept going.

And when we were out on the street,

10   Ziggy jumped up on strangers, delivery people, everyone.
When I said, "Down!"
Ziggy just wagged his tail.
Mama would look at Ziggy and say, "Bad dog."
Which made me sad because

15   every night Ziggy slept next to me,
soft and warm, kept me company
And every day greeting me home from school with
a jumping hug and a thumping tail.

20 Mama sighed, "One more person he puts his muddy paws on
or knocks down and that is it.
It's time for the running off
to stop, too. He needs to come when you call
and stay down when told."

I didn't like "that is it." So, I made it my goal
25 To train Ziggy.
Mama signed us up for dog school <u>obedience</u> class,
so Ziggy could learn to do as he is told.
The people and dogs practiced walking together
with a pat on the head for stopping
30 And "Down boy!" listening.
There were not many pats for Ziggy.

Ziggy and I went to class after class, more time than most,
And no matter how many times Ziggy just walked away
I called him back, and back, and back.
35 And then one day he did
Come back! Every single time.
Then I said, "Stay!" and walked away.
He sat. And sat. And sat.
Until I said, "Come here."

40 That night, the delivery person came
To the door. I answered with Ziggy starting to
raise up until
I said, "Sit." He sat. Just like that.

"Good dog," said Mama. Ziggy thumped his tail
45 And smiled his doggy smile.

1. The poet uses a comparison in line 3 to help the reader understand —

   A who gave the speaker Ziggy

   B why the speaker was given Ziggy

   C what Ziggy looked like

   D what Ziggy liked to do

2. Which of these lines from the poem best helps the reader know what obedience means in line 26?

   F I didn't like "that is it." So, I made it my goal

   G so Ziggy could learn to do as he's told

   H The people and dogs practiced walking together

   J There were not many pats for Ziggy

3. Which of the following lines from the poem contains personification?

   A he ran toward the waiting hills and tangled woods

   B jumping hug and a thumping tail

   C He sat. And sat. And sat.

   D raise up until

4. What is the main theme of the poem?

   F It's important to have a pet.

   G If a goal is too hard to reach, you can adjust your goal.

   H Family members should support and help one another.

   J Working hard and not giving up can help you reach your goal.

> **Quick Tip**
>
> If you are not sure what a question is asking, reread it and underline or circle details. Think about those details as you reread the text to find evidence to answer the question.

EXTEND YOUR LEARNING

COMPARING GENRES

COLLABORATE

- In the **Literature Anthology**, reread the narrative poem "Stage Fright" on pages 138–139 and the folktale *Blancaflor* on pages 118–131.

- Use the Venn Diagram below to show how the two genres are similar and different. Thinking about genre characteristics will help you compare and contrast the two different genres.

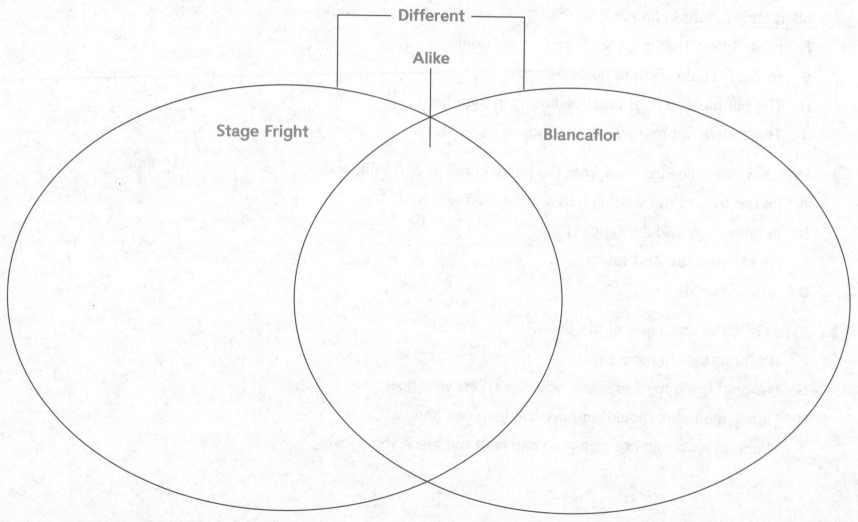

Different

Alike

Stage Fright

Blancaflor